THE OTHER SIDE OF REASON

A JOURNAL ON PTSD

DAVID B. GIBSON

Library and Archives Canada Cataloguing in Publication

Gibson, David B., 1962-, author

The other side of reason : a journal on PTSD / David B. Gibson.

Issued in print and electronic formats.
ISBN 978-1-927032-51-0 (paperback).--
ISBN 978-1-927032-52-7 (pdf)

1. Post-traumatic stress disorder. 2. Gibson, David B., 1962- -- Mental health

I. Title.

RC552.P67G53 2016   616.85'21   C2016-904940-X
                                      C2016-904941-8

© 2016 by David B. Gibson. All rights reserved.

No part of this book may be used or reproduced in any manner whatsoever without the prior written permission of the author, except in the case of brief quotations embodied in reviews.

All author royalties from the sale of this book go directly to Carleton University scholarship funds set-up in memory of both Connor Boyd and Kyle Nash.

Cover: dreamstime.com autumn-grunge-2955819.jpg © Barbara Helgason

Design and editing:
Peter Geldart
Danielle Aubrey
Petra Books
petrabooks.ca

Disclaimer: This journal hopes to raise awareness and provide knowledge of the complexities surrounding PTSD; there are passages that may be distressing to some readers. The book is for informational purposes only and is not intended to be a substitute for professional medical advice, diagnosis, or treatment.

Here's what readers are saying

"I often say that there are no accidents. That everything happens for a reason, the good, the bad and the in-between are all part of our path. How we live with it, through it, learn from it, and the choices we make as a result of it define us.

It's hard to fathom that the events of that fateful September day unfolded with such devastating loss of life, lives forever changed, that it was in anyway meant to be. How does this happen? How can anything like that have meaning? Families torn apart, people struggling, as David teaches us, every day. David and the other people who were on the bus or lost loved ones on it are faced with the daily struggle of finding meaning with that day and then every day beyond it. How do you transition to simply coping to healing and finding yourself again? Is it even possible?

For David, healing comes in the raw, personal and deeply intimate journals of life after everything changed. We are privileged to be given a glimpse into his personal, daily struggle; the anger, doubt, fear, confusion and the impact it has had on the ones he loves most. The courage that comes from his experience may be David's 'meaning', or at least the beginning of it, unfolding for him. If his experience can spark an understanding about trauma, and open a dialogue to others who also never expected to have to deal with it, perhaps the train may be silenced. The reality is, that it may never be, that is the sad irony of healing, sometimes the journey is life long, what we do with it to regain power can define us, and sometimes that power becomes our greatest gift."

— Peggy Taillon

"You may think you know someone. You experience a side of a person in the context of your interactions, your communications or your observations. But, do you really know that person? We are shaped daily by our experiences, each episode changes us, but do we realize that? Each encounter good and not so good impacts who we are. But do we know this, do we accept it and learn from it? Do we really know ourselves? And, for some of us, do we want to know ourselves?

...

Here's what readers are saying (continued)

Suddenly and unexpectedly our world can change, and, with it, we may change. David, quietly and with a degree of somber reflection, shares his journey to accept what may be unacceptable. His challenge to accept and not judge his struggle is articulated in a clear and concise manner as he reveals his feelings and lets us all into his life. Thank you, David."

— Wendy Talbot

"This is an intimate and candid portrait of the raw emotional wounds created by sudden and shattering trauma. David's poetry and reflections over many months capture, with palpable authenticity, the anguish and burden of a survivor. We see glimpses of a man grappling with a surrounding world which, by its normalcy and relenting ordinariness, is paradoxically and unyieldingly hurtful and alienating. Readers have the unique privilege of sharing elements of an unimaginable journey through this remarkable and powerful collection."

— Isra Levy

"When a master builder approaches a new project, he takes many things into account including the materials, the worksite, the environment and the desired function and aesthetic of the project. If he is wise, he employs a principle of learning and adapting throughout the entire process — as the project progresses, some materials may become available, the site may experience physical changes, or new conditions may be brought to light.

As I read my friend's journal entries, I am reminded of this iterative design-build process. As David constructs his bridge from where he has come to where he is going, I witness him examining the foundations, assessing the raw materials and looking at the veiled bank where he is heading. I also see him looking down into an abyss and struggling to reconcile how the bridge will relate to this chasm.

...

While David's writing illustrates the early days in the construction of this bridge from his head to his heart, I am filled with admiration for his courage, because like all bridges, his is not meant for just one journey, and through sharing his story, he removes any toll for others to walk this bridge with him."

— Robert Walsh

"Reading about David's inner journey took my breath away. His coming to grips with the horrific accident that oh so suddenly became a part of his life's journey, left him spinning in an inner world of such profound anguish.

David's words so poignantly capture the struggle of someone so desperately wanting to get over a deeply traumatic event; wanting to get beyond the nightmare to a place where he could put himself back together again.

This narrative of his painful journey lights a path for others dealing with trauma. His reflections are truly those of a wounded healer."

— Jack McCarthy

"Powerful, humane, dark, torn but not beaten, and not finished. When you might want to stop fighting, I won't ever let you. The belief that you can overcome this is in my heart and in your family's, and my hope is one day you can close this chapter. Your power and strength, and the will to be the victor on this journey is empowering to me, your family, and to those that are trying or going through the same struggle. Your message is clear, moving, filled with sadness, fear, and of the battles with your nightmares. It's a journey to the end. No matter how long the journey, you will persevere and will always have the support of those around you.

You have already conquered more then what most will ever have to in this lifetime."

— Luc Fournier

Continued after the Epilogue...

This book is dedicated to my family for holding onto hope. To my wonderful wife, Tammy, who has shown me she'd stretch her soul just to form a constellation to light my way home. To our four beautiful sons, Joshua, Matthew, Justin and Colin, who constantly remind me of how proud I am to be part of their wondrous journey in life and just simply being their Dad.

Part of my journey of healing is the continued support and understanding from others that while not all injuries are visible, they do matter just the same.

Acknowledgements

I want to acknowledge the continued faith, love and understanding from my in-laws, Don and Brenda, my mother, Carol, my sister, Cathy, and brother, Craig.

I am indebted to the Board of Directors and staff of the Sandy Hill Community Health Centre who have given me the chance and support for my recovery to begin.

In memory of my dad, Hugh Gibson, who taught me the meaning of adventure and the tranquil path of the canoe.

My sincere thanks to all my colleagues and friends who acted as the 'preview readers', and whose comments are included within this book. What an honour to have your first reactions — Peggy, Isra, Wendy, Robert, Jack, Luc, Hersh, George, Eric, and Tim!

Thank you to Dr. Larry Cebulski for writing the Foreword in this book, and being a guide on my pathway to healing.

This book would not have been possible without the expertise of both Robert Walsh and Cristina Coiciu. I am forever grateful and honoured to have you as part of this journey.

Finally, thank you to my editors at Petra Books who worked with me on this endeavour.

Memorial Funds at Carleton University

The Author's royalties from the sale of this book will go equally to two Carleton University funds set up in memory of both Connor Boyd and Kyle Nash, two students who were killed in this accident.

If you wish to contribute a donation please go to the Carleton University fund-raising page for:

(1) the Connor Boyd Memorial Fund at

futurefunder.carleton.ca/giving-fund/connor-boyd-memorial-fund-giving/

and/or

the Kyle Nash Memorial Scholarship at

futurefunder.carleton.ca/giving-fund/kyle-nash-memorial-scholarship-giving/

(2) Click "Donate Now".

(3) Fill out the rest of the form accordingly to complete your donation.

You will receive your charitable tax receipt in the mail.

Thank you.

"Upgrade this to a mass casualty...I have one, two... six code blacks."

— First responder

"I always have this tension between the drive to bear witness to the impossibility of successfully conveying the traumatic experience, with the strong urge to repress the experience entirely."

— David B. Gibson

Gibson

Contents

Foreword by Dr. Larry Cebulski..................vii
Preface..1
Introduction..5

    Chapter 1..9
    Chapter 2..21
    Chapter 3..37
    Chapter 4..49
    Chapter 5..61
    Chapter 6..77
    Chapter 7..109
    Chapter 8..127
    Chapter 9..159

Epilogue 201

References to illustrations and passages................211

Foreword by Dr. Larry Cebulski

For most of us, the events in our lives are predictable. They make sense. Occasionally, this predictability is interrupted by exceptional events that give pause, and may create strong emotional reactions. The vast majority of these experiences fall well within our mental model of how the world works, or how it should work, and of our place in it. That is, while exceptional, these events still make sense.

Sometimes, events occur that do not fit into our conceptual view of the world. These events may violate our sense of fairness or justice, such as an unfair accusation or an inconsiderate act. Or our sense of personal safety may be interrupted. On these occasions, our emotional response may direct us to correct the situation, to right the wrong, to fit things back into our model of how things are supposed to be.

And, then, there are experiences that not only don't fit our model of the world, they destroy it. These experiences challenge our moral viewpoint or our individual self-portrait, or threaten our existence in a way we can't reconcile with how things are supposed to be. We are unable to right the wrong. Our reference points are lost, and we feel vulnerable, frightened and disoriented. When we try to re-orient ourselves, we find that we are unable to. The once familiar pieces of the jigsaw puzzle of our reality no longer fit together. Some pieces are missing, and, what's worse, someone added new, and different pieces we can't recognize. What was familiar now seems foreign, unreal, and dangerous. What was meaningful no longer has meaning. We feel threatened where we once felt comfort. Even in our sleep we feel threatened. Our behaviour changes in an attempt to cope with feelings we do not fully understand, and in so doing we become incomprehensible to our friends and loved ones. Our efforts to cope and to understand hurt those we love the most. In this way, they too become victims.

David Gibson's reality was altered in a moment on September 18, 2013. His eloquent and poignant requiem chronicles his efforts to re-orient himself to a world whose boundaries and reference points abruptly disappeared. In his poetry, he chronicles his experiences in a way that helps us understand the hidden struggle of Post-Traumatic Stress Disorder, or PTSD.

March 2015

Preface

Imagine a bright sunny September morning. Imagine walking to a bus stop thinking about how your day will unfold. Imagine a day like any other day as you board your bus. Imagine your bus leaving the station like it has for as long as you can remember. Seconds later, three things happen at the same time. The rail crossing lights are flashing with a train approaching. People are yelling for the driver to stop, and the bus driver maintains his speed approaching the rail crossing. Usually, that's not normal. Now, imagine being on this bus that is not stopping. Then, impact. Life was over. Life is over.

So here we are. You and me. And my story.

How then can this tragic accident be expressed to find a way out of my suffocated self? What are the different ways to deal with the persistent, horrific images, to grasp the elusive aspects of such a traumatic event, and thus move beyond what is inexpressible?

Story-telling from one's traumatic experience is frequently in precarious territory. It is emotional for the story-teller. It seeks understanding to elicit personal change while at the same time, attempting to convey to others the experience of surviving in a way that imparts that understanding. This intersection requires the author to explore that which is often considered "unpresentable" and reconcile his need for visual distance with a desire to stir a reader to empathy, understanding and even engagement. Reality-informed adaptation in story-telling is by definition in touch with 'the real' but it is only a copy, one version — One's version.

Honouring such tragedy means striving to understand and convey the significance of the event, while recognizing the impossibility of grasping that significance or its impact on me or possibly the others who were on that bus.

In our lives we usually have a sense of what is to come — a constant point of view on progress. The crash changed that for me — it just happened, and life is supposed to go on — but no one prepares us for this kind of life interruption. It shatters our sense of order and thrusts us into a world forever changed, like a state of perpetual disarray with a lingering sense of unease and disorganization.

The traumatic experience not only forces me to question or abandon my more superficial assumptions about myself and the world, it also threatens my core assumptions. These are the very assumptions that organize our experience of, and relationships with, our self, others, the world and the human condition itself.

My hope is that by sharing my experience of the accident I can also inspire people who survived the accident to have the courage to speak out loud and not suffer in silence or in shadows. I never thought I would ever experience such trauma or the after effects that continue to interfere with my life and my family's life. In the end, I realized that I needed to find some meaning from what happened.

This collection of journal passages is the story of my journey after surviving a horrific crash when a double-decker bus slammed into a passenger train in Ottawa, Ontario. From my perspective as the author and as a passenger on that bus, my story is a place in time. It is a place that holds the experience of what happened, but it is also a place for me to visit and set down my feelings for reflection and examination, not for pity or to feel sorry for myself. This is a beginning, of sorts, but I am unsure as to the ending.

— David B. Gibson

The Other Side of Reason

Gibson

Introduction

In his 1974 Pulitzer Prize-winning book *The Denial of Death*, the psychiatrist Ernest Becker proposed that much of what characterizes our humanness — our culture, belief systems, sense of self and belonging — is shaped by our need to offset the inevitability of dying. Survivors of traumatic events are brought face-to-face with this reality, and they must find ways to temper it, to assure themselves that their lives count for something.

Living through a trauma can take a terrible toll on our lives. It's debilitating, it's exhausting, and it's frightening. Once the dust has settled, everyone's lives slowly return to normal. It's assumed that the traumatized person will likewise be able to put the trauma behind them and move on. But many carry the effects of trauma through the rest of their lives. Sure, they adapt, and do the best they can.

But life is never quite the same again.

The sad truth of the matter, is that each and every day senseless things happen to people who are just trying to live their lives the best way they can. Trauma does not discriminate nor care if you are a good person or not. Out of nowhere it can strike, leaving a trail of shock, disbelief and shattered remnants of the person you were. The sheer randomness of the trauma can unhinge you from what the world was, to a world view that challenges every belief you held. Trauma at its core, creates a loss of faith that there is any safety, predictability, or meaning in the world, or any safe place in which to retreat. It involves utter disillusionment.

When we are in danger, it's natural to feel afraid. This fear triggers many split-second changes in the body to prepare to defend against the danger or to avoid it. This "fight-or-flight" response is a healthy reaction meant to protect a person from harm. It is common to experience upsetting, distressing or confusing feelings afterwards. The feelings of distress may not emerge straight away — you may just feel emotionally numb at first. After a period of time, you may develop emotional and physical reactions, such as feeling easily upset or not being able to sleep. This is understandable, and many people find that these symptoms disappear in a relatively short period of time.

But in post-traumatic stress disorder (PTSD), this reaction is changed or impaired. People who have PTSD, may feel stressed or frightened even when they're no longer in danger.

Essentially, the brain constantly records memories on several different pathways. The conscious path allows you to remember episodic and semantic memories—those you can picture (like your favourite flower) and those you have learned (the capital of Canada is Ottawa). But there are also unconscious memories, which can be thought of as our experiential emotional learning. These memories might give you a feeling of discomfort when you remember the smell of a skunk that sprayed your dog, the sight of a doctor's needle, or the sound of a dentist's drill. When you survive a traumatic event, this emotional learning kicks into overdrive — your memories tell you to respond in the future the way you responded in the past. You're alive and survived, therefore whatever you did or did not do during the event, worked.

The other effect of a traumatic event is that the amygdala — the part of your brain that controls your emotional responses — is triggered. Whenever something stressful happens, from a stubbed toe to a loud noise, like a fire alarm going off in your building, your amygdala activates your autonomic and endocrine systems, releasing stress hormones and neurotransmitters such as norepinephrine and glucocorticoids. Normally this is a good thing: these chemicals usually persist in your body for minutes at a time, allowing you to react quickly to harm.

But extreme events can leave you permanently primed, with raging stress hormones.

Being diagnosed with PTSD, I learned that it is really an anxiety disorder caused by a traumatic event and characterized by many of the symptoms I was presenting. Symptoms like reliving the traumatic event through nightmares, flashbacks, and intrusive images of the accident and aftermath. Other symptoms were feelings of emotional numbness, the feeling of being on 'edge', depression, anxiety, angry outbursts, irritability and panic attacks.

Post-traumatic stress disorder I discovered, is trauma on steroids.

There's no time limit on distress, and some people may not develop post-traumatic symptoms until many years after the event. Additionally, not everyone who has experienced a traumatic event develops PTSD. The thing about PTSD is that it's not just a memory, it's feeling like you're back in that horrific event and it plays out over and over again. This is something that is not easy to deal with, much less live with.

Gibson

Chapter 1

"I found a place no one should ever go;

I am not the person who is standing before you, I am the silent one inside..."

—David B. Gibson

I am here. I wait.

I think of the lake.

I imagine something mysterious rising to the surface on a bright autumn morning.

For an instant it shows itself and is gone before I can comprehend it.

I do not point, nor shout, I would not dare. After all, I could be wrong.

By the end of the afternoon, the shape — whatever it was, I can barely remember. I cannot be made to state it was absolutely thus or so. Nothing can be conjured of its size. In the end, my sighting is rejected, becoming something only dimly thought of — dreadful but unreal.

Thus, whatever rose toward the light is left to sink unnamed; a shape that passes slowly through a dream.

Waking, all I remember is this awesome presence; a shadow, lying dormant in the twilight, whispers from the other side of reason. I am here. I wait.

September 2013

Two seconds

Cars stopped.

Cross lights flashing.

Train.

Cries — "Please, stop!"

Still moving? No, it can't be!

I am seeing, but not believing.

In slow motion — tragically unreal.

"Stop!"

Terrifying sounds, images trapped in an instant.

Two seconds.

Two seconds is all it took.

October 18, 2013

Into the darkness

Take my hand, son, and walk with me.

Shadows guide me through a moonlight serenade of a thousand slivers of light.

'Where are we going?' I ask.

Somewhere — nowhere — where time watches the fading light of sorrow.

A tragic veil of reflection is revealed.

I step off into the darkness — free falling.

And then, a soothing rapture of nothing wraps around me.

Sleep has finally found me.

Finding me

Where are you?

I'm outside, looking in.

Vaguely familiar, almost translucent,

Travelling to anywhere but here,

Faces race by, out of focus.

Eyes that look past, but not within.

A touch to know I am real.

But where are you?

In the river's morning mist,

Flowing in an infinite journey.

Something I cannot hold onto, nor stop.

I am lost.

Losing myself

The hurt — I see it in their eyes, I feel it in my heart.

No looking back now — what is done, is done.

I don't think so — the sadness remains only a heartbeat away.

Inside, an illusion of strength and a reminder of quivering weakness.

Taking hold of me, I lose myself in a flash.

Unsure of who I will become.

More scared of who I am to those I love.

I see it in their faces — my own reflection — what is done will always be unfinished.

Breakaway solace

In Times Square I feel safe among the thousands of strangers who walk by me.

My story is lost among the nameless humanity.

I am caught up in the neon lights of a New York minute.

It's funny how I can feel secure when my son feels so overwhelmed.

Is it because I have started to give in? To stop fighting?

I am angry with myself for not being able to get over this.

I feel like people think I'm being dramatic. I don't know if people understand that I don't want to be sad or miserable either.

The nightmares that come during the night drain me of hope.

During the day, these flashbacks seem to come from nowhere — sometimes unsettling me.

These pictures in my mind should not be a part of me. These memories, suffocating my spirit, hold me so tight I can hardly breathe.

I found a place no one should ever go — I am not the person who is standing before you. I am the silent one inside...

Lady Liberty, bring me home safely.

In search of feeling

I dream of a yellow rose bud ready to blossom, but then plucked off its stem, frozen in an instant, forever in time.

Slowly, as if coaxed back to life, the yellow rose bud begins to open, revealing the boundless beauty within — a rapture of colour and scent — something to behold.

It holds the promise of hope, captured and sustained forever, like the many pictures of roses in my home.

Somewhere, through the numbness and sorrow, there dwells a single yellow rose, waiting, searching.

I remember, but want to forget.

Until then, I feel like a castaway on a deserted island. Hoping beyond hope that I will be rescued — that I will return home safe.

Waking, I look out my bedroom window not knowing, nor wanting to know.

For a new day will always remind me of a single yellow rose.

November 2013

The other side of reason

Fluttering wisps of light reach through the darkness to awaken my blank stare;

Leaves swirl around me with a faint chill of the autumn breeze.

Unbelieving, my eyes focus on snapshots of time. Images that stand still for eternity. Cruel and relentless like dreams gone by.

Blinking, I try to bring focus through tear drops of pain and sorrow.

I am unable to understand, to even fully comprehend, what is in front of me.

Darkness, once again, finds me — 'Where are you?' I ask.

I am always here — waiting, watching.

But I can't see you — I don't want to see you.

Wiping away the mist, my vision returns.

I see the mirror never lies.

Lament for hope

I watch the gentle descent of snowflakes blanket the cold ground outside.

Transfixed within the moment — like the ice cubes swirling in my glass.

A time to escape, a time to not feel pain.

How long, I wonder?

For now, I rely on her gentle hands to hold on, for me and for us.

November 18, 2013

The Other Side of Reason

Gibson

Chapter 2

"The Trauma said, *Don't write these poems. Nobody wants to hear you cry about grief inside your bones.*"

— Andrea Gibson

In search of truth

I am in a space of pain, loss, struggle, sadness, anxiety, intense frustration and anger.

I am holding onto a sense of tenuous hope in the face of self-honesty and introspection,

And it all feels a little closer to the truth.

A little closer to telling the truth.

To others,

To myself,

To the part in all of us that tries to close our eyes to what we know to be the painful truth.

Help me make it better.

And when it does not, and you cannot, it may be after a time when it's too late.

And we are comforted, for but a moment.

My story helps us to take a deep breath, and to say to ourselves: it is never too late for him.

December 2013

Meaningless unmasked

Our need to protect ourselves is an illusion when we know we cannot.

I have no time for words to fill in the spaces.

No way to know they know.

I am stuck on this side of reason — trying to find meaning when there is none to be found.

I remain stuck, spinning in losing myself.

Finding meaning only when by remembering who I once was.

Bus stop 4608

In the 386 steps from my home is bus stop 4608 I used to think about work, or if we needed groceries...

Now, my steps are less assured, almost hesitant.

I think about my family farewells, hugs and kisses — did I remember to say I love you?

With every step, a painful memory of what was in time a bright autumn morning.

Now, I walk to uncertainty.

Waiting for bus route 76.

Gulf coast oasis

Florida sun and white powder beaches bring me to an oasis — a pause in time.

Christmas is here with a silver tree encased with a hundred lights to sparkle on our lives.

A seagull cries overhead while the sun touches our hearts with its warmth.

Waves chase the shoreline as my footprints trail behind on the ocean's edge.

Laughter and smiles abound — tennis and runs into the cold surf.

Hope and faith restored — captured for eternity within our hearts and minds.

I want to believe again — the promise of better tomorrows,

Of a Merry Christmas and a Happy New Year.

Mind ghosts of time

Lost in myself and stranded in time.

Trying to find a sanctuary to hide from the past memories that haunt me.

Unanswered questions — with no reasons as to why the unthinkable happened.

I sit alone, replaying a loop of unnerving nightmares.

Slipping in and out, it seems my mind knows no rest.

'Please stop!' I will always hear them cry.

Whispers of voices — only for an instant.

Captured for eternity, the haunting silence of lives lost.

December 18, 2013

Black shorts and the abyss

A powerful and heart-breaking image haunts me to this day.

At the edge of the upper level of the bus rests a pair of black shorts.

Lying among bits of glass, perfectly laid out for all to see.

Where once there were seats, people and an upper glass window, there is nothing but open space.

How odd that a pair of shorts is all that remains among the mangled and twisted front of the bus...

I wonder where they came from and whose they were?

But then I look down among the wreckage and shudder with fear.

What a surreal moment, horrific and tragic all at once.

January 2014

Idle time

With dread and with fear I await the stillness of night
and the quiet moments of the day.

Without the distraction comes the surging tide of dark
images.

I feel the panic swell up in me like the bitter taste I have
in my mouth.

Trembling nerves and cold dampness surrounds me.

Like a caged animal, I pace back and forth endlessly —
going somewhere but not knowing where.

I have nowhere to run or hide.

The shadow of darkness has found me once again,
and holds on tight.

The fog

I feel like I am lost in a fog.

Like my feet are stuck in sand at the water's edge.

I am desperately trying to find a way out.

Exhaustion becomes my only respite.

But only then, the faint rumble of the train comes heading my way.

In my mind's eye

When I close my eyes, I see the train coming.

Squeezed shut, I see again the shattered forms.

Of screaming people, a separated arm and lifeless bodies,
   just lying there for the dawn of reality to find.

Of shattered lives, shattered minds, shattered hopes —
   from so many lives.

Into the abyss I try and hide, to protect myself
   from this scene,

Where the tears of fear run down my face.

For in my mind I have built this place of anguish.

Perhaps one day, I will be set free.

January 18, 2014

Time tracks and transitions

Just breathe.

In the silence of a cold winter's night,

The vapour of my breath rises toward the dark skies,

Only to disappear without a trace — just like...

Time is as fleeting as it is unrelenting.

Only five months have gone by.

People have moved on — Why haven't I?

Depression and loathing masked by medication.

It's been a long winter, indeed.

February 2014

Why me? Why *not* me?

A debt owed.

Separated only by fate.

One family's loss, another family's relief.

It just doesn't seem right — it could have been anyone that autumn morning.

I beat the odds — others did not.

Am I worthy? Am I deserving?

In the meantime, I keep their memory alive as I struggle to make sense of what happened.

To make sense of something that I will never fully understand.

Unanswered observations

Two letters ahead of the final Transportation Safety Board Report.

My stomach tightens with anxiety.

Patterns emerge to a seemingly random accident.

Is this a tragic chain of preventable circumstances?

My heart races, I feel sick reliving the crash all over again.

I am filled with impending dread to the unanswered questions.

What does it matter in the end?

After all, observations have already been made.

Observations to the questions that will never bring them back.

The echo of memory

In solitude, the sun sets before me.

It is as though the person I once was has vanished.

Those that surround me do not understand
    where I have gone.

I am clouded by misunderstandings, frustration,
    and a fight that I am not winning.

The flashbacks come and the nightmares stay.

I am waiting and praying for the light of day.

The Other Side of Reason

Gibson

Chapter 3

"PTSD is a whole body tragedy, an integral human event of enormous proportions with massive repercussions."

— Susan Pease Banitt

The guilt proposition

I know guilt is a choice but I feel powerless — I am here.

It's as though I feel guilt for being alive, when others are dead.

I feel guilty for what I cannot do, and for what I cannot undo.

It is an irrational guilt, but that makes it no less powerful.

This guilt is all consuming.

I get up every day and go to work, but I feel as though I am sleep-walking through my own life; at times, my guilt feels like a bottomless well.

Will I ever feel anything other than sadness again?

March 2014

Dreamscapes

I feel a deep and subtle panic take hold, the definite sensation of an impending threat.

And in fact, as my dream deepens, slowly and deliberately, each time in a different way, everything collapses and disintegrates around me.

The setting, the people, the sounds, while the anguish becomes more intense, and more precise.

Now, everything has changed into chaos.

I am alone and confused in the centre of a grey nothing.

And now, I know what this dream means, and that I will always know it.

March 18, 2014

The escape artist

Trade winds, sun, warmth, sand and the gentle lap of waves surround me.

A time to take refuge and feel again.

To see her beautiful face, her smile, her gorgeous blue eyes and feel her gentle touch.

To play without thinking.

To see again how beautiful my boys are.

So much time I have missed.

I am thankful to have — my life, no, our lives, together in this Caribbean dream.

The new normal

I am told my responses are *normal*, on the journey of healing.

I hate the word 'normal'.

I hate the way I feel about myself; self-doubt, anxiety, lack of confidence.

Feeling self-assured — where has it gone?
    Where has it all gone?

The nightmares that will not stop.

The growing intensity of anger and frustration that lies within me.

This is my new normal. This is the darkness.
    This is what it is.

Nothing more, nothing less.

Suffocating in silence

I feel like I have lost my edge.

That spark in life that ignites me, and motivates me.

It's like I have lost my place in life.

I am hiding inside myself, struggling to find some measure of balance and truth.

The tragedy is that I have so much to say and offer — to myself and to others.

April 2014

Mist-covered fields

In the early light of dawn, I step into the dew-covered clover field.

Only stillness surrounds me. Morning has broken with a slight chill to the spring air.

The mist hangs low over the field, clinging to the sun's filtered rays.

Are you another shadow in my life, grasping at the awakening day?

Another scar you simply fade away. Where are you now?

Eternal. I will never see. You are just a dream — so lost.

Forsaken, all for naught, and even mistaken.

Out of the morning's light I turn and walk away.

Aftershocks

Where is the calm when there is still no answer? We wait.

Outside are the echoes of a roaming storm of uneasiness, fleeting and uncontrolled.

The dread of wanting to know the truth and not knowing how to comprehend the truth, when we may already know it.

Indictment and blame are becoming more pronounced as does the awareness of my rising anger.

At the same time, we wait for, and avoid, the answer to the question: why did he not stop?

Harbours of healing

Sail away to somewhere — to anywhere.

Sun-kissed golden tan with baby blues under the Oakleys.

Sounds of laughter and island music vibe.

The Caribbean with its turquoise sparkle.

Swimming in the sunshine without a care.

Under the stars and in your arms of love
we dance the night away.

A repose in tropical, sunshiny days —
to feel alive together.

The promise of spring

In the light of the early spring morning, I am yours.

Will you walk forever by my side?

Will you stay forever in my life? For I am weak.

Alone I cannot face the future.

I need your strength to make it through the darkness.
    Together.

The promise of spring will be my shining light.

April 18, 2014

Dark skies

My eyes keep silent as everything passes through my mind.

I exhale and let go.

Another nightmare.

Another reminder that nothing is as it seems.

I'm so tired of being scared awake.

Always the sound of the morning train.

I'm not sure I can do this anymore.

Riding the 76, or even any bus for that matter.

It's like I am going through the accident all over again.

May 18, 2014

Gibson

Chapter 4

"Some people's lives seem to flow in a narrative, mine had many stops and starts. That's what trauma does. It interrupts the plot. You can't process it because it doesn't fit with what came before or what comes afterwards."

— Jessica Stern

The doorway

I just want to stop hurting inside.

The crash still seems so recent, like a mountain that is far away but that you can see clearly, because it's so huge.

I flash back to that terrible autumn moment.

I don't want to live my life being constantly scared. People don't realize how life-changing accidents can be.

I've been told, "You look great. Why can't you move on?" But it's like a part of me died, and I have to start life all over again. A different person.

What I saw was horrifying, but it doesn't mean I am crazy. Letting myself feel what happened has partly helped me become unstuck from the accident.

It dawned on me the other day that I continue to hurt because I am feeling so out of control.

What I need to realize is that *no one has control of the present but we can open new doors to our own future. As one door closes it doesn't mean another won't be there for you to open.*

There's a bottom line that life can be dangerous and there are no guarantees.

I realize I can't control everything, and I need to find the things I can have a sense of control of.

In the end, it makes me more mindful of how I want to live, and the new person I hope to become.

June 18, 2014

Tomorrow's resolution

I woke up this morning with that fear that just envelops me like a big heavy blanket thrown over me that I cannot get out from underneath.

I keep looking back with sadness and pain, and revisiting the crash, again and again.

The pain is a cry for a resolution of sorts.

So I can let it all go.

Close the door.

Turn the page and move on.

This is what I want. What I hope for.

I want this beginning.

Sleep walking

The thing is, from the outside I am functioning and doing the things in life I need to be doing;

Going to work, riding the bus, going to the lake to be with friends, being a father, son, brother, friend and husband.

Inside my head is an ongoing struggle to keep it together.

I still can't stop the nightmares and my mind still seeps with images of the accident.

The accident permeates through me like how a flu makes you feel.

So, on the outside, people see who they think they want to see.

But inside though, I am still trying to cover my eyes and block out the sounds.

So I don't have to feel the ebbs and flows of fear, pain and sadness.

July 18, 2014

The paradox of moving on

To talk about it is to feel the panic swell inside of me.

To be silent about it dishonours the lives lost and diminishes what I feel.

Everyone wants to move on and to lay to rest the past.

I want to, but I cannot.

'Enough!', is what I see in their eyes.

If it were only that clear and simple.

Looking back to see tomorrow

There is a saying, 'just because the past comes up from behind and touches you on the shoulder, doesn't mean you have to look back'.

Memories can't be so easily forgotten, however.

Your mind's eye is not so easily deterred.

Nightmares have a way of clouding your tomorrows;

They are always a reminder you will be touched by the past.

August 2014

One of the nameless survivors

As I approach the first year anniversary of the bus crash, my thoughts and prayers center on the families who lost loved ones.

I often think about the many people who lived through this tragic experience and wonder how they are coping today.

How many have moved on?

How many will never be quite the same?

I often think about wanting closure, but I am unsure of what that will mean in the end.

Or whether it will even make a difference.

August 18, 2014

The coming realization

I think it's safe to say that the worry and fear I felt on extremely bad days would return, was always just lodged at the back of my head, banished and silenced in the hopes that it could stay buried there...and eventually just fade into non-existence. But, as I have learned, that's not the way it works.

I am discovering that trauma will always be there with you. It will come, and it will go, as regular as the tides.

The emotions and memories will always be a part of me... and will always somehow be a part of my family's life.

With trauma I hold in a lot of anger. It is a free-floating anger with no real target and very subtle triggers. It simmers below the surface and can jump out at inappropriate times, aimed at the wrong person for the wrong reasons.

Suppressing this leaves a horrible feeling.

In between somewhere

The passing of time.

Moments we live and lose.

Days or our lives?

Does it make a difference?

In the loving and our embrace.

Or in the dreaming of what could come to pass
   and what could be passing us by.

Near or far from here.

Like the tide and the moon's calendar.

Somewhere.

The Other Side of Reason

Gibson

Chapter 5

"Forgiveness is giving up the hope that the past could have been any different."

— Oprah Winfrey

The hurt

"I can't do this anymore", she cries, curled up on our bed.

Hiding the truth to shield me — judgement day has arrived for us both.

It was inevitable that something, or someone, would have to give.

I guess I never knew the extent of the hurt I caused.

I stare expressionless, not quite grasping what I now know to be the real truth.

I walk away feeling numb and not knowing what to say — but realizing the hurt goes both ways;

Hers, suffering in the shadows, and mine, in silence.

September 2014

Making amends

His father's frantic phone call — I shiver with dread.

I already know what he will ask me before I answer the call.

"Was he on the bus?" I can hear the controlled concern in his voice.

"I can't be sure", I answer — but in my heart I am sure — he was at the front.

I went to the Sportsplex to see his mother — to offer my comfort and to wish for the miracle I knew might never be — I needed to be there for both of them.

Her eyes knew better — a mother always knows.

Please forgive me for not telling you.

In silence, I will remember

I started my journal almost a year ago — a reflective journey of sorts.

I have since traveled to a place that will leave me forever a different person.

I realize I will never be that same person as I was prior to the crash.

I have learned that time has a way of dulling the emotional intensity, but my nightmares a year later are still a constant reminder that the past is never too far away.

I wonder how many others live in silence a year later.

But for today, my thoughts will go to the families and friends who lost their loved ones that autumn morning.

Please let us never forget.

September 18, 2014

The answer

Distraction, and a mere 7 km/hr is the Transportation Safety Board's 'qualified answer'.

So many of us have waited for this moment for so long...

What a horrible answer — a 'preventable accident'.

Perhaps, it would have been easier to accept if the driver had suffered a 'medical incident'.

The answer tears at my heart, and leaves me with a deep sense of sadness and anger.

There is no relief, no closure, from the answer.

It seems my life will always be a waiting game.

The key hole

A year later, I said I was finished writing.

How could I have predicted that this terrible journey of recovery would be far from over?

Of course, for many, the past has been buried and put to rest with the passing of the first year anniversary and the release of the Transportation Safety Board Interim Report.

Life has a way of moving on — not waiting for anyone, especially those who are lost in time and trapped within their traumatized minds.

September 18, 2013, has become a footnote to the back pages of yesterday's news. There is now little patience or appetite to continue to talk about what happened on that bright fall morning.

But in my head I am overwhelmed by the messed-up thoughts that come without warning — I am still not okay. Feeling isolated to fight your demons alone is never a good thing.

I long to find a way out. That tiny light I can still see through the key hole.

My key to that light is to continue to write.
And so, my journey continues...

October 2014

The deconstruction of David

I characterize last year's tragedy as an 'experience of the impossible'.

The frailty of life sunk in with my acute awareness of my own and others' mortality.

I am left standing paralyzed, mute and solitary.

I am trying to unravel my illusive truth to reveal the contradiction of who I was before with who I am now, and with who I will become tomorrow.

There is something inside of me that is trying to understand, but I don't understand.

The images I see are constantly in front of my eyes.

Each time I get on a bus, which is about twice a day, I watch the bus I am riding crash into a train.

I can't avoid seeing it — this is my deepest and darkest anxiety.

Can I reach a place where I can reconcile the tragic consequences of the crash?

Will someone else's eyes ever see what mine see?

Or, will this forever be the 'impossible'?

Glory bound

And the night begins to crumble and drain away, giving way to dawn.

Life's questions are suspended and replaced with a gateway to Caribbean self-discovery.

Let us disappear and reappear to reawaken our senses and our love for each other.

Travelling to a new world we have never been in — with a story we have yet to write,

Searching for what is true — to find a little more peace of mind, joy and solace in our lives.

The moon's light washes away my fears and leaves no trace.

A time for us to be lost together in the moment of a lasting embrace,

My arms holding you so close — I see the smile on your face and a twinkle in your eyes.

The warm rays of the sun — to see this world ever-so beautiful,

From the darkness, into a bright light of hope.

I just want to feel the warmth of your love so close to my soul.

The ripple effect

She describes it as the 'face of withdrawal',

The switch that has been turned off — but I don't even realize it.

And, once again, they retreat from me.

They have become witness to another person they call 'Dad', but don't understand.

I have become unpredictable to them.

I have become that someone else I don't want to know.

How they see me, or react to me, is understandable — I just never knew.

Somehow, I get lost within myself and say and do things that are hurtful.

And, sometimes, I just don't know who I am anymore.

Left behind

The November air is cold, and dusk has descended.

In the distance, a street lamp flickers and, far away, a rumble of an approaching train awakens my thoughts and makes me remember.

At times, there's only blackness and confusion inside of me.

The blackness is hard to describe, as it's more than a symptom. It's an all-or-nothing.

An all-encompassing and unsettling feeling that repeats itself over and over again.

A wave of unimaginable despair sweeps into my life — just for one key moment — and wreaks such havoc that, in just an instant, my whole world will never be the same again.

Part of me is seared into place.

The rest of me moves onward, dealing with all the *todays* and *tomorrows*, but something, some part of me, is left behind.

That part blocks the light, shades the rest of my life but, worse than that, it continues to be alive and imposing.

I feel trapped forever at that precise moment.

Left behind to face the nightmares that come back for more.

November 2014

Hold me tight and never let go

I hate getting flashbacks from things I don't want to remember.

Sometimes, I find it easier to keep silent than to tell you just how I am feeling,

So I write to release the pain, the anger and frustration I feel.

I know in my heart that you can hear my words, but I worry you will not understand what the words mean.

I imagine that my words will someday help you understand why I am the way I am — a world that is too frightening to believe that I am even inside — a world that can hold on to such pain and fear.

I don't want to push you away — but I imagine you are scared of the words I write down.

So I live with a sense of desperation to know if you will be there by my side and in my arms.

To live with this struggle — a struggle that shouldn't have happened to either of us.

The numbing effect

There are the times I wake up feeling like I don't have any emotion;

There's an emptiness, a void that takes me away to a place where I am neither happy nor sad.

I can hardly understand it but it feels emptier than anything,

Like you can't feel anything for that moment — leaving the darkness to fill my mind.

But, slowly, the light starts building back up.

With the smile of my waking wife, and her face that I know shows me she still cares.

I am really trying my hardest to stay positive and present.

Although my demons lay quiet, they are never quite silenced.

I have yet to learn to confront them and, certainly, I have been unable to run from them.

I never wanted to be like this.

The slow dissolve

My edge of darkness — it comes in the night from which my nightmare binds the stars together in the heavens above my head — heavy and repressive in its own darkness, neither emitting nor absorbing light.

I am neither here, nor there.

I am without a past, present or future.

I wake up a lot seemingly trapped within nightmares, caught in a fog I can't get out of.

So I'm constantly trying to figure it out — the 'it' being what happened and what's happening, and a little bit of what will happen.

I long to find some calm within the *who* I have become.

The Other Side of Reason

Gibson

Chapter 6

"There are wounds that never show on the body, that are deeper and more hurtful than anything that bleeds."

— Laurell K. Hamilton

The unexplainable

People think, "It happened, so get over it!"

They think someone can go through something like this accident and get over it.

It's like when you remember something negative, like breaking up with a partner, it stays with you for a while. The accident is like that but much worse. It plays on your mind constantly. It doesn't turn off.

It's complicated to explain to people. And for most people they don't want to listen or hear it.

I have what I call my 'empty' days. Days when I am locked in a feeling of nothingness. Like I am walking through an empty dark hallway just trying to reach the doors at the end and walk out into the light and fresh air. Not a bad mood, not exactly happy either. Just there.

How do you really explain the unexplainable? I become exhausted just trying. It's a constant struggle.

Part of it is the exhaustion from trying to make sense of all that goes on in my head.

The other part is that I fear going to sleep — this is the worst. The nightmares, my brain not shutting down, the chatter and noise that occurs when it is dark and there are no other noises around is scary.

My head has created a prison and I can't figure out how to get out. It is a vicious cycle, the less sleep I have, the more irritable I become, and the angrier I am with myself and the world.

Sleep has become my enemy — it means my nightmares are almost upon me.

December 2014

Hoping for hope

Moving through the cold, hard, unflinching darkness, toward the light.

"Will I ever forget?", came my anguished cry.

The answer I hear: "No, you won't. This is part of you. It will always be with you. But it is what you do with that memory, that knowledge, that understanding — what you do with it is what matters."

I describe my circumstance as a 'condition of dis-control'. A life of nightmares, worry and high anxiety.

Take an average person's full-blown work stress and multiply it by ten. It's being agitated the whole time.

The very basis upon which I have built my life has been challenged — by one single event.

What happens is that dreams can become nightmares, joy can become anger. The world that was once safe can just as suddenly feel very unsafe.

Living through the effects of the accident is often talked about in terms of symptoms and treatment, but sometimes it doesn't align to the depth of what is going on. It's about my identity and trying to re-engage in a new world.

One of my biggest fears is that I will never be right again.

My hope is that the difficult things, whether it be depression, sadness, fear, anxiety or anger, will just go away.

I may have times where I feel overwhelmed and I don't necessarily know why; times that are worse than others and feel completely random.

The truth is, I still remain unsure of who I am.

The challenge I face due to the accident is a challenge to the limits of myself, my humanity and how I view the world.

The mask

Away from the world, my tears are unseen.

I smile for the world, yet inside there is blackness like I'm sitting in a room with no lights on.

My words become frozen upon my lips.

I am becoming terrified of my own mind, so I am quiet most of the time.

The mask that I wear is a stop gap — a way to distance how I am feeling with the world.

This mask is like putting on a front to hide from what the truth really is.

Sometimes I forget who I am beneath this mask.

It can't be me — can it?

In a perfect world

Have you wondered what it could be like when there is nothing there?

Conversations that are locked away in your mind?

When in a tranquil moment of time our reflection flickers from the candle's warm light.

Mirrored through our touch and into the heavens above.

In a perfect world, we are not always what we promise to be.

That shine on Christmas night

Does it feel like Christmas?

As the days slip by I start to disappear from the light.

Can my soul still fly among the falling snowflakes — just a whisper on the breeze?

Simple joys that will make it feel like Christmas once again.

Tree decorations that weave a tapestry of our life and love together.

Can I be still?

The warmth of the fire, the glow of the tree lights.

My spirit still rests among the moonlight.

Your loving smile, your gentle face.

Peace is the rapture of Christmas.

Hope is what waits beneath the blanket of snow.

Timeless melody

How everything has changed.

Within the stillness of winter's touch...

The quiet hush of snow floats gently all around me,

My chilled breath forms a mist lost to the morning sky;

Behind me, the songs of the chickadee echo among the cold gusts of wind,

Drifting to another field afar, their sounds slowly fade away.

A melody for life lies only a heartbeat away.

Behind the frosted window pane I see my family waiting.

Dreaming on the edge

Imagine that you are able to dream when you are awake but can't tell that you are dreaming.

Now, imagine that you had something bad happen to you. From then on, you find yourself transported back there to that time.

The bad thing just happens over and over again in exquisite detail.

It's like a dream in that it isn't actually happening but just like a dream you don't know that it isn't happening.

That's what happens when I am awake.

January 2015

Time goes by

The faces, the connections, and the places I have seen.

The point of no return and the lessons I am supposed to learn.

Forever in my mind. I will always see you.

Someone out there knows me, a reflection in time.

All that is done. My eyes are still wide open.

I am patiently waiting.

Through the window of a new day

Those moments you lie in bed, wondering how you're going to get through another day, putting on your best face and going to work.

Then the moment when that unreal reality sneaks its way through and leaves you unsettled.

And you try to lose yourself in the responsibilities of work, 'till another reminder finds its way in.

Pushing your way through the fog and uncertainty, you carry on — one hesitant foot after another,

One new day at a time.

Where have I gone?

I see my past — one day is all it took — stolen away.

Inside is my pain — what is wrong with me?

Where is the old me? Where have you gone?

How could this happen? This person I have become.

I wonder how long this will last. Where is my sense of believing — in something, in someone or even myself?

In the meantime, I will keep searching and trying to find the person I used to be.

And then, hopefully, one day I will wake up.

Believing I am the person you see in front of you.

From the air — the overhead window

From the sky, I see the tragedy laid out with blue, white and yellow tarps.

Among the wreckage, the silenced voices remain.

From my vantage point, I know that they were once alive but now will lie still forever.

I have to find a way to build significance and meaning to my life, to help me forge a path in a world that hasn't changed along with me.

I am trying to do this in opposition to the consequences of the accident — the ongoing intrusions and roadblocks that I stumble over.

My sudden anxiety that can occur for no apparent reason, an enveloping wave of anxiety that makes it difficult for me to think, reason or act clearly sometimes.

Getting a decent night's sleep remains a continuing challenge. Fatigue often becomes my constant companion spilling over into many areas of my life. The fatigue is physical, mental, and emotional. At times, I feel wrung out, as my temper shortens, my frustration mounts, concentration lessens, and moody behaviors escalate out of nowhere.

I am still plagued and often haunted by unwanted and continuing intrusive thoughts and memories of what happened.

My memories keep coming at any time of day, but more fiercely at night, in such excruciating detail that I feel like I am reliving the crash over and over again.

Looking upward, I know there will be no answers to realize — just the endless blue sky.

Brighter days

With another new year upon us, someone remarked that there would be brighter days ahead.

"Have faith in yourself", they said. I smiled back with a nod of my head — my eyes staring past them.

Funny how all I want to do is run away.

There is something to be said for denial, you don't have to feel your nightmares for a while. It's like a pause in time, brief as it may be.

Denial is like waiting for a chance to feel alive again, it sets my soul free and cleanses me of the past.

I'm still looking for the courage to stand against the fear that rests among my memories.

Fear can undo even the best of us, but I also know it can teach us a lot about ourselves.

"Everything you want is on the other side of fear" wrote George Addair.

My journey is to try and get there.

Kiss of dawn

The sun rises on my sleeping meadows, making the flowers bloom with the kiss of dawn.

Butterflies follow my wandering soul, with my eyes watching the sky unfold.

In the soft kisses of the sun.

Good evening, Mr. Darkness

Our good byes are not supposed to be final farewells.

So much we take for granted in this life.

As days struggle into weeks, and weeks turn into months
— time sharpens the anguish.

Can you hear their screams?

I feel like I am stuck in a long hallway of mirrors,

Each one shows something different and unfamiliar.

I can't even tell which one is me, but I know you are there
— I can see you within my own reflection.

Your tightening grip twists me from the inside out, letting
me breathe just long enough to remain conscious of
every fear and pain you unleash.

The Other Side of Reason

You bring me close to the ledge of oblivion only to wrench me back just so I can experience the fall — over, and over again we repeat this unreal nightmare.

I know this won't get any easier, and for now I know it won't end.

But I am getting stronger and wiser to spite you — all thanks to you.

Waiting for the day I will become my own light.

By my side

In the darkest of night, midnight tears flow.

Dawn breaks gently, sunlight filters through.

Chasing away the grey.

Walk with me across the sand, beside the gentle sea.

Hold me close.

Please don't let me go.

February 2015

Facing toward the sun

As the light faded into darkness and the night sang the soft lullaby,

I drifted again to the beginning. Or was it the end?

Sometimes, I fall deep into the abyss of my shadow.

Larger than life, it engulfs me.

And I forget...

All I have to do is turn around and face the sunshine.

The wind in the night

In an old growth forest, on a certain night,

Writing thoughts.

Sometimes it's like trying to catch the wind.

Or holding hands with time.

You think you have a good grasp.

But then you turn to look.

All you can see are the trees that cast shadows
by the moon's white light.

It's like a cold breeze that slices clean through your
mind.

Watching, and waiting.

From the shadows between the trees, you emerge —
a beacon of sparkling light.

In this life, it is always good to find a safe place
from the night.

Fallen

Some nights, the sleeping memories wake.

And I free fall from the hanging swing of the moon.

I have been brought to my knees once again.

And so I shall do what I am supposed to do, something I have never done, something that will change everything.

I shall not question 'why?'

In the quiet moments of reflection

"It shouldn't be this hard", she told me one evening.

She continues with lips trembling, "Sometimes I am so angry with the fact that they got to at least grieve for the passing of their loved ones, but I have to live with the accident every day."

I say I'm sorry a lot — knowing that 18 months later we are still fighting a battle that is up for grabs.

I know we can't go back to life as it was before.

I continue to go through therapy to understand the how and why, and go through prayer to obtain absolution, but I still can't turn back the clock.

I also know she is waiting longer than she thought she ever could for this to end.

I need your light

Somewhere in the western sky, just below the setting sun rests the truth about the lies we tell ourselves.

How do you light the way when it's been dark so long?

I need your light — I can't do this alone. I can no longer cry another day.

I am more than you can see. Stand beside me, don't be afraid.

But in truth, I am lost in my fears. I have no more sense of these days.

I have little fight left to feel.

I need your light, because it's you who can see us, and who can shine bright our love song.

The gate at the end of the path

It was a tired patch of weathered ground at the end of the path. An old wooden gate was all that was left to even know this place existed — back and forth, swaying to the wind the gate would creak. No one ever went there, why would they?

Sometimes, when it felt like it was getting bad, more silence than anything, I would disappear down there, to the end of the path, where the creaking gate welcomed me. I would sit on the grassy knoll, feet tucked up against the moss covered rocks, knees jutting out, kicking stones down the hill. With every tiny stone I always felt a little bit better, a little bit braver ready to suck it all up and head back up the path and appear at my own front door.

So, that day, I sat there. And I waited. I could hear it all, the dinging sound of the rail crossing, shattering and spinning — echoing around my head as clear as ice. The swaying back and forth as the train cars sped by.

Stones couldn't help me. Neither could the words
I had no time to say.

I had nowhere to turn, to get away from the noise.

So, I concentrated on my horizon, on the old wooden gate, and the path homeward — pleading for the old wooden gate and path to guide me away from the wreckage, an escape route into the unknown.

But no train came. There was no escape. Another bad memory inside my head.

The night wrapped around me quickly and completely, like a dark blanket, suffocating me with its thickness.

This time, the mist of time hid the gate at the end of the path — there would be no stones to find.

Even my tired cry couldn't save them.

All it brought was a train taking away whoever was in its way.

The windows flashed past in the early evening darkness. I didn't feel like jumping up and down and waving.

So I just stood there and watched.

Push it all away

Something I don't talk too much about is my ongoing back pain from the crash.

The horrible part of my back pain is that it serves as a reminder of the crash.

It has become a silent and, at times, an intrusive reminder for me that my life has changed from the way it was before.

Physical pain, I have discovered, can be pushed away out of necessity. At times, it feels like I have lost my physical well-being on top of all of the other stuff going on inside my head.

Sure, physio and pain meds can relieve some of the pain, but it hasn't resolved it. Before the crash, I was active and in good shape. Today? Not so much.

The Other Side of Reason

In many ways, the crash left me unable to control my life — which has become unpredictable — completely random in some cases — but not in a good way.

I used to believe you made your own best luck by what you did in your life — like working hard, being honest, or helping others less fortunate — the crash changed all of that.

The crash has left me playing with a new set of rules — ones I don't even understand or want to engage.

High Stakes

I have often been asked: "Why do you continue to ride the bus when so many others cannot? Does it not remind you of the crash?"

My response is far from certain — I believe for some of the passengers, they will never ride a bus again. Everyone reacts differently, depending on who you are as a person.

For me, it's been like living on a razor's edge — one side continues to relive the crash, the other side is about who I am as a person — it's complicated and frightening all at once.

To stop riding the bus dishonours those who survived and the memory of those who perished. If I stop riding the bus, then I am giving up on who I was, who I am now, and who I will become tomorrow.

This side of the razor's edge battles all of the impacts of the crash.

To give up is to lose my life.

It is not a question of choice.

It is about my very survival.

Staring the dragon in the eye

I've tried to do everything I can to push these awful memories away.

In the process, I am still trying to gain a full realization of the impact and the meaning that this crash has had on my life.

I like to use the analogy of 'I'm staring the dragon in the eye'.

I will have to someday confront this shadow, the darkest place inside of the dragon.

This inner search will have to tame the beast inside of me.

I need to lift myself from the unconsciousness of my darkness to establish some control over my life.

I don't think there is a cure for what I am talking about.

I'm talking about living and putting myself more in touch with my life and emotions, on good days and bad days.

I have to teach myself that I can live with this and live a valued life — a life I want.

How am I doing? I don't know yet. That's the honest answer.

Gibson

Chapter 7

"Trauma destroys the fabric of time. In normal time, you move from one moment to the next. Sunrise to sunset, birth to death. After trauma, you may move in circles, find yourself being sucked backwards into an eddy or bouncing like a rubber ball from now to then to back again. In the traumatic universe, the basic laws of matter are suspended."

— David J. Morris

Invisible reflections

It seems not long ago. A time and place I had been.
   A summer haven.

With the fading light of the evening's red summer sky,
   I turned toward the peaceful lake and the distant
   shoreline.

Sometimes, the water is so still it sparkles from the glass
   surface. At other times, the raindrops cause little
   pools of reflection that break the surface of the water.
   Each droplet of rain circles a ripple out ever wider
   across the lake. Across my life.

The mirrored surface of the water may, at times,
   be broken by leaves and debris, and yet the whole
   remains complete.

It is very difficult to see ourselves as others see us.

Some people choose never to see themselves in the
   mirror.

I see my reflection in the mirror as an expression to
   the world. A face that does not tell the entire story.

A story which remains incomplete.

March 2015

Release and control

Steam rises from the hot water in the tub.

I do not feel the cuts that slice my stomach.

But I do feel the pain trapped within my mind.

I watch as the water stains red.

Slowly, I feel the release. It's like a calm that drifts over me.

I feel in control once again.

I live for a moment that makes me feel alive.

Afterwards, I feel horrified and revolted by what I have done. The shame is overwhelming.

I worry about how you will see me — totally insane.

The shirt hides the truth. Now comes the worry.

Will you ever understand?

Split lives

Desperation cried.

Night wore on, colder.

In the space between dreams and reality, I feel lost.

My life feels divided between two different time spans.

Before September 18, 2013, and afterwards.

I feel like I am holding on to a part of me that is no longer there.

Why did this happen to our family? Why could something this awful happen to anyone?

What I'd give to have never been on that bus. To have been even just two minutes late would have meant me missing the bus entirely.

Two minutes and the living nightmare, gone. Two freeing minutes being 'normal' again.

It's so lonely being stuck in this life now.

Just for me, however

These crazy thoughts rolled through my mind as I tried to find anything and everything that might bring any kind of relief from the memories that are overwhelming me.

The lingering effects of the accident, literally feels like it is shredding my mind into pieces.

So how am I supposed to navigate this trauma?

The best I can. The worst I can.

I remind myself constantly that in this moment, with the incredible pain and fear I have been left to handle, I'm still here and I'm still trying.

It's the best I can do.

Pressing the mute button

Sometimes, the invisible injuries are the ones that leave the worst scars.

I feel like I'm not moving on the way I thought I could.

I've been struggling to understand what lesson could be taken from this tragedy.

Then there is the hard task of putting on my 'masks' and pretending that everything is okay; that's a draining thing to have to do all the time.

Yes, I'd love to say "No, I'm not good at all. I'm struggling so badly at the moment". To be honest, I just want to crawl into a ball and sleep this time away. But I don't, I just smile and say "I'm doing okay, thank you, how are you?"

Even everyday activities are hard. I think I have to do this, that, and the other thing, but I either forget or once I start doing something I get so distracted by my thoughts that I stop what I'm doing or forget what I'm doing in the first place.

Sometimes, I just have to watch the world go by, and let it all go.

Finding sleep

Memories should be about things that warm your heart, but they may also rip you apart.

Eighteen months later, I am finally rediscovering what sleeping is.

I have finally been given redemption from my nightmares. Almost gone is the terror that triggers my waking panic and sweat-soaked shirts.

The trepidation of going to bed, which turns into an ongoing escape from the inner darkness that follows me into my awakening moments of fear and pain.

I am slowly releasing myself from my night companion — of being constantly on guard, tense, and on edge.

Sleeping for me has meant losing all control.

I finally have a fighting chance.

The light from within

My family's like a stained glass window that glows and sparkles when it's sunny and bright.

Together, we step into a Caribbean paradise.

A time to discover what truly matters. Hand-in-hand, we are complete again.

The vista is lined with majestic palm trees swaying to the rhythm of the ocean breeze and the many tropical flowers with their kaleidoscope of vibrant colours.

I can taste the salt in the air from the ocean.

Your smiling faces and sun-kissed hair shines with the rays of the sun.

I love you with all that I am and all I hope to be.

April 2015

The way it's going to be

You and me, both.

I know we have seen some things.

Like the cold sun of the autumn that sets on where we have been.

And I know it makes no difference that I am in too deep.

Keep moving with me now.

I know it's the way it's going to be.

Just keep moving.

The waking dragon

My journey since the accident feels like I have been through a labyrinth of many dark shadows that envelope me.

I believe that to wake the dragon is to confront the recurrent, uncontrolled, and intrusive painful memories of the traumatic event.

I feel I am only touching the edge of healing, often plunging into unknown and forbidding places.

Perhaps this is where my life is to start over again. To find a new meaning to my life against the backdrop of who I was before.

Is this waking of my dragon a new transformation of who I will become?

Will this journey ultimately be about better understanding the many emotional layers of a traumatic experience?

For now I know that the waking dragon will always be with me, surfacing without an end in sight and reminding me of the pain and fear that still resides within me.

May 2015

Morning bloom

I can feel a presence rising from within and the thoughts bloom like pink dawn poppies.

Seductive and fragrant.

I feel the morning air lift me.

My eyes meet the gaze of the spring sky.

Let me fly to meet and follow the winds' call.

Or will the scents just suddenly disappear?

Watch me tumble and fall.

Dissolve like nightmare traces as you wake.

Is it fear or courage to be dismissed at dawn's arrival?

Are these just memories which keep me aloft or dreams that almost come true?

Time warp

People ask me, 'Were you on the bus that crashed into the train?'

Yes, I was there last night. I was there this morning. Five minutes ago, before you asked me. And I will probably go back there tonight.

Trauma can warp one's sense of time, making weeks and months flash by while one remains partly mired in the past. This untethering from time is unsettling, because it is a persistent reminder that one's life is different from the people who are 'normal'.

Trauma is in many ways a disease of time.

To this day I still have traumatic memories that communicate an uncanny feeling of timelessness.

This place I only know too well

It's wretched here.

The damp fog prevails.

It's cold as well.

My heart can't seem to warm up.

My thoughts live a life of their own.

That fine line between hope and despair.

But this place is distant in the depths of my mind.

It is never a question of travelling to this place.

For when all is said and done, it's not 'if' I will go, but 'when'.

To be free

Time has become a weapon, wielding pain with every tick of the clock. I feel each minute. The sun goes down without notice and I no longer greet it when it rises. I feel like I am hiding myself from the world.

I have ended up becoming the person I need to be when I am around people so that they will not worry or think that something is wrong. I still have to deal with the demons that often flash through my mind without warning.

It is during these times that I am extremely aware of everything that my brain is firing at me. The fact is, I don't feel like I am getting better, and I am not going to ever be the same. Each day is a testimony to how much I care and love you, suffering as quietly as possible so that you can feel as though I am still here for you. In truth, I am nothing more than a shell, filling space so that my absence will not be noticed. Yes, in truth, I have already been absent for a long time.

The trauma I still feel causes me dread and agony even with the medications I am taking. It seems there will be no cure, only the masking of the anxiety, depression and fear that lies just beneath my cold skin.

Relationships feel stagnant like when you are away at school for many years and then come back a different person — everyone else it seems has moved on without you. Activities I once enjoyed are now dull or even unimportant.

But far worse is the numbnes I still feel. I can barely stand getting out of bed. Everything simply comes down to passing time until I take my medication to shut my mind down and try to sleep again. It feels like I am drifting without a purpose through my waking hours.

To be free again is a false hope reserved only for dreamers.

June 2015

The perfect storm

The crack of thunder and lightning lights up the night's dark sky.

Pouring out the sky's own sheet of stinging tears.

Winds blow cruelly tipping the fragile balance of life.

There is no warning nor premonition of what is coming.

Today I can still hear the faint rumble of the storm's distant fury.

The Other Side of Reason

Gibson

Chapter 8

"Everything you do shows your hand. Everything is a self-portrait. Everything is a diary."

— Chuck Palahniuk

Open book

Passing through the autumn hue.

Carry on, I'll bear this scene.

With each flicker of moonlight the silence settles in.

Torn and tattered the pages flap to the night's lonely breeze.

I guess the book was written, two years ago.

And I said things, I should've kept to myself.

I fear this book will gather dust.

But I can't let go somehow.

For this is the sad irony of a story being lost.

June 2015

Autumn flashbacks

My first flashbacks were more like a sickening awareness of the crash still to come.

When the flashbacks are triggered, I suddenly feel very unsafe. I feel cold, damp and shaky, and I get a sick feeling in the pit of my gut. I feel anxious and frightened.

Then, the emotions come like a flood gate. Whatever emotions I have repressed along with the accident wash over me, and I feel as if I am drowning in a sea of terror and grief. The anger always comes later.

I never lose touch with reality when dealing with the flashbacks. I am always aware of where I am. The flashbacks seem like they are part of me, like I am reliving the memory of that autumn morning.

The hard part is always dealing with the aftermath of the flashbacks.

For days after each flashback, I have to deal with intense anger, terror, and sadness. I don't think it is the flashback itself that bothers me the most: it is the lingering despair and pain that comes with having the flashbacks.

Blinded

I'm blinded by it. I can't seem to see my way through or out of it.

It comes and goes to varying degrees but is often times not only blinding but paralyzing. There's no short-cut I can take.

My thoughts are so random and scattered that I can't seem to focus. I'm just feeling weary of it all. And it's not something I can turn off. I can't snap out of it. Or willfully distract myself from it.

I'm continually trying to make sense of it all. One thought leads to another, then they all get mixed up and the next thing I know it's tomorrow and I go through it all again. I have accomplished nothing for the day.

I now know that it's not a sign of weakness on my part to share these feelings, but beyond that, I don't want to hurt those around me by letting them know how much I'm actually hurting. By letting them know how lost I really am.

What I still don't know is how to make it stop... how to work through or move past it.

The lingering effect

For the moon, you see, shines only at night.

Why then does the coldness linger?

Don't ask too many questions. They might find you.

Words I dread and a truth I am fighting.
    What the future holds, is difficult for me to say.

I am afraid that I'll never be there. I had hope,
    but it was cast aside.

My dream of never awakening

Living with trauma defies all rational arguments, appeals to "get over it", and any deviation from the vital course of self-preservation. It feels like living inside a cocoon.

The root of trauma I am discovering, is that the brain is fighting an opposing battle, pitting the experience of the past bus accident against the present day's 'safe' reality. I believe that trauma disperses the worst aspects of my lived experience of the accident to infect everything I do and see today.

I don't feel the same and this part of my current reality seems to be inescapable. There is fury at the tragic minutiae of daily life that remains long after the crash.

I am left struggling with this debilitating, relentless condition and I have lost more than I ever knew I had. The contemplation of how to live after such a traumatic experience is so impossibly tied to the landscape of my life that it requires a rearrangement of my identity.

'Are you going to be okay?', is what I keep hearing. This is a deceptive question, and one I'm not sure how to answer.

Crystal ball visions

The colors of seasons change. This window of my life shares a story of where I have been. Looking for something. Searching.

Hoping to reveal the very answer to the questions of my pained soul.

Ready to run away into the new season of life with a cautious spirit.

In this story, I may have to face this road alone and its narrow path suggests just that. For my soul needs to get away.

My eyes need to gaze upon a new life. I need to feel the wind blow on my face.

A portal to my soul that opens and closes just as fast as lightning strikes. And to see I must really be looking.

Searching for that one chance to get a glimpse of something so powerful, so deep.

To embrace it. Embracing this hard and well worth season of discovering the real.

Of discovering myself.

August 2015

Truth or dare

I have found that keeping a journal is powerful in the moment we write — it allows us to put our thoughts and feelings outside of ourselves and get objective distance from them.

Sometimes writing in a journal is a way of processing or purging a traumatic circumstance — we can feel cathartic and somehow cleaner on the other side of our writing.

I have also found writing to be powerful when our former self is the challenger, talking through the very words we put to paper.

It's very hard to hide from the truth as we know it and told it.

If of course, we're willing to tell the truth and hear it.

One day again

I see the morning come quickly.

Do you believe in this life you have been given?

Do you know the reason you're counting on me, or yourself?

Your life has gone by fast. Are you afraid to know your name?

Keep on living. I've seen you giving up inside and waiting for your life to begin.

Your life is a hideaway.

You can't hold it back.

You will be okay, there will always be another day.

The story of bearing witness

Alicia Ostriker once wrote, "Writing is what poets do about trauma. We try to come to grips with what threatens to make us crazy, by surrounding it with language."

So how does one honour and remember the tragedy of September 18, 2013? How many candles does one light? How often does one pray? Do we know how to remember the victims, alongside those who survived?

The journal I have been writing, is in many ways, a silent witness from that time and beyond.

I have also experienced the excruciatingly painful task of testifying to the trauma, pain and grief with all the personal courage I could muster.

It seems to me that to fall silent in the aftermath of this tragedy is to surrender to it. How can one ever write about this event? A more important question that I have explored with my recovery, has been, 'how can one not'?

When I first thought about sharing my lived experience of the crash, my hope was that my words would reach others who were on the bus with me, and possibly touch their inner lives about what living through trauma can look like. But as time went by, I found that my experience was really a story within a story which was much broader than just me.

Two years later, I still believe that my experience of trauma will somehow be heard, and bring us to a place of encounter, empathy and faith. In rediscovering faith, I am learning that it helps me to gain a better understanding of who I am, trusting and allowing things to be right again. Restoring faith has also been a difficult and painful journey.

September 2015

Sunsets and sunrises

Forever, we floated on the water's surface unafraid of where the world might take us.

For a while we forgot our time...

I can feel the wind coming in off the lake.

Not a whispering wind. Not the gentle breeze that comes with daybreak.

My hair is damp with the secrets the waves just couldn't stand to keep a moment longer.

All the things they wish they hadn't seen, and all the hope the waves wish they knew how to give.

These blue eyes hold so much pain.

The Other Side of Reason

So much darkness.

I finally see this and it tears at my soul.

And I'm trying to reach you as fast as I can.

Can't you see me in the mist? Of course you can't.

But you can feel me.

And I'm hoping that's enough.

To give me a chance.

To get into the light.

And grab hold of your hand.

Acceptance of the unacceptable

PTSD is a feeling; the experience of being submerged in a reality that is entirely unreal to the reality others are experiencing. I feel this is like a punch in the stomach that never stops landing. I feel shaken, like the ghosts are screaming at me to do something and I can't move a muscle. It's too late. I'm too late.

Experiencing PTSD isn't linear. It isn't something that can be controlled. It isn't clear and concise. And, above all else, it isn't in any way, shape or form, simple. It's a strange line to tread. A shaky, contradictory balancing act. For me, it's these uncomfortable contradictions that living with PTSD brings, and what makes the impact of PTSD so unbearable to live with.

PTSD feels vast, and deep; even two years after the crash, I still have not found the edges of feeling 'normal' again. I stretch out thinking that perhaps if I reach far enough, I will find a place inside where it ends, but, so far, that has not happened.

I've been giving myself a hard time for finding this recovery process so difficult, and for not getting over it. I keep telling myself "it's been two years David, come on, accept it and move on".

But, what if what happened, was so unacceptable — so unforgiveable.

How does one ever reconcile and find acceptance?

I struggle with my life a lot of the time, but I love the people who are in my life enough to keep going. I feel so thankful for that.

All I can do is to keep my life jacket on and remain afloat.

I can't always look down into the depths of the ocean. I have to look at the sky. The giant sky that is there for me to take in.

When swimming becomes too difficult, I just float. There's my acceptance.

Living the myth

It is a pivotal and an excruciating moment when we realize that we cannot protect our family from any tragedy that may impact on our lives. This is even more acute if it is ourselves.

Today more than ever, it feels sometimes like we have been bombarded with events that remind us of this heart-clenching fact. One of the hardest things I have ever had to experience is letting go of the myth that I could protect my family and knowing there was something even harder yet to come.

For my family and me, the dissolution of this myth began on September 18, 2013. I had two sons in high school, two others living on their own and my wife at work. The tragic collision between the bus and the train in Barrhaven, sent me reeling as I could not find a single reason why I could have ever been in harm's way as a passenger on that bus, nor the contemplation that my family would have to live with that horrible moment when they realized I was on that ill-fated bus.

Like any person involved in such a horrific event, for months I was haunted and felt raw on a visceral level. I think that feeling of near death exposure came from letting go of the illusion that, even though my family was innocent, even though they were encased in a world designed to ensure their safety, such safety could never be assured. Knowing something and experiencing the realization, for me, were two very different things.

I believe my children and wife still either believed that such horrific events would not come into our lives, or that if they did, that as a father and husband, I could always offer them protection from such pain and tragedy.

But then I heard it. In between phrases we have all said to each other, "I can't believe this. It is just so horrible," was the painful recognition that I was on the bus and that we might never be the same as a family again.

The hardest day was not when I realized that I could not protect my family, it was when they did.

Letting go

It was cold where I was, and when I tried to open my mouth to speak, no words could emerge. "Let go of the past; accept the present, and have faith in the future" he said in a calming and soothing voice. Standing in the church, my tear-filled eyes could not see past the stained-glass windows.

I turned toward the big oak doors crossing into the threshold of daylight, leaving the Minister standing alone. I glanced back, and as our eyes met for that split second, his expression showed both concern and surprise.

It wasn't long after my wish for the Minister's absolution that I realized that when I let go of the past, I would also let go of myself. But how much of what I let go is essential to my being alive?

Without my past, will I simply fall over when I try to walk forward in life?

Finding peace within myself may mean letting go of life's expectations in order to avoid the disillusions. Perhaps my absolution to moving forward.

On change and loss

It's September. The end of summer, the start of autumn. The month when nights start to overtake days. The darkness keeps on seeping in, evening after evening, and with it, the fading of all summer memories, those shiny evenings and days full of possibility.

Now it seems null and void somehow, a vague far-off memory. And I'm left miserable and moping, trying, but failing, to find my feet in this new seasonal landscape.

The seasons of course have their own reflections in life. I feel it because I have lost someone — my possibility within this season of change.

And with that, the season creeps in as a spectre I suppose.

On finding meaning

Living with PTSD is perhaps the pinnacle of the lie we impose on our separation from what we consider to be 'normal', with what marks someone as a person who is considered something less than anybody else.

The prevailing attitude I have in dealing with this experience are feelings like; 'I should suck it up; and just get over it'. Unfortunately this is where my feeling of shame comes into play.

The shame I hold as someone who is living with the impacts of the accident, arise in part, because I think others who went through the accident must be doing just fine or have had it far worse than me. Somehow, I feel I don't measure up to what I think many believe as something anyone should be able to get through and move on from.

So "learning to deal with it" doesn't quite make sense to me. It's learning to heal from it, not deal with it, that reflects more accurately my experience of recovering from the accident.

Two years later, I am still not feeling 'quite right'. Through it all I've had full support from good friends and my family. My wife is the best; she is awesome in her patient help and love. My lads have been understanding and so far more than forgiving.

I also have my writing. It makes me feel better somehow. In a way, this is a form of therapy for me. It's a good way of getting these thoughts and feelings out of my system. This is why I write about my experiences. I'm not trying to seek attention, nor am I after anyone's sympathy and I'm certainly not looking for a pat on the head.

Writing helps me share my feelings of what it is like to deal with the aftermath of a traumatic experience. For me, finding meaning from this tragedy has become a pivotal part of my journey in healing.

Sometimes sharing one's writing and experience may make a difference in someone else's life.

In and out of focus

Without realizing it, my eyes gradually start to lose their focus. The trees become a swaying green blur and the coffee mug is merely a white smudge on the brown wooden desk.

It's weird. Looking but not seeing.

And there I sit, motionless. Staring.

Time passes. The clock ticks.

Maybe a minute passes, maybe an hour, maybe a whole morning.

And then I become aware of someone's voice. Distant and muffled, it sounds so far away. As if I have my hands over my ears.

With a shake of my head I force my eyes to focus again and turn to see someone looking at me from the doorway. 'David'

At the same time as my eyes refocus and my ears start hearing clearly, I realize there is a large lump stuck in my throat. My chest feels like it's in a vice and I momentarily panic that maybe I'm having a heart attack. Is this what is feels like to have a heart attack?

Please no one come over right now...

My hands are shaking uncontrollably, and I can feel the muscles in my belly twitching and jittery. It's sore and frightening. Every muscle in my body is tight, shaking and tiring. My energy is sapped by these muscles, leaving me with barely enough strength to draw in another breath. Breathe... breathe...

Time passes as I focus on my breathing. Surviving.

Eventually it passes, the shaking slows down and the pain eases. Total exhaustion! Every muscle is sore and fatigued, there's nothing left. The lump in my throat reduces to being merely annoying and uncomfortable but no longer restricts my breathing.

I get up from my desk with no concept of how long I've been sitting there.

Time is non-existent.

Touchstones

Never let go. Let's leave this world behind.

In the darkness with each other's light.

In the moment we've always known, and in the valleys of our touchstones.

Is this the vision we will share?

If the truth be told I'll never be the same for sure.

It's easy to say there is nothing in here to see.

Just look into my eyes and I can trace my life into your precious light — just for your love.

We have nothing left to loose, but all our dreams left to find.

I will find them with you.

October 2015

Humpty Dumpty had a fall

Imagine you are a beautiful, much-admired, hand-blown glass vase with exquisite colour and form sitting on a fireplace mantel.

Now imagine being in a horrific crash as the beautiful glass vase gets knocked off the mantle and smashes onto the floor.

Most will rush quickly to gather the pieces and try valiantly to piece it all together, with anything they can, so it will appear like it used to be.

But there is no way to do this of course.

The moment

Oh it feels colder, have I lost my innocence in a journey inside? Was it only two years ago?

I woke today, cast in blue. I keep pretending it will get better over time.

Losing the sounds of where I am, there is no soft landing.

I would rather be here.

We've come so far you and I, we are an echo of reflection together.

I close my eyes and look inside. You have arrived, the endless beautiful face behind my eyes.

And now's the moment to let go of every battle that weighs me down.

To open my mind to all my worries and all my dreams.

I am a witness to being one with all I am. Take a glance at this mystery.

I don't want to float away.

The road

It seems I walk a lonely road when I am deep inside,
yet you are never far away.

I'm heading out to see the light. I'm heading out to see
this world.

My vision is out of sight to the answers I need to find.
I just might never know.

What's our future going to be? All the light is fading,
it's like the night is craving for the silence of an
empty road — slowly I am moving while I keep on
dreaming of a place I haven't been before.

Maybe I will choose again a life to begin.

The winding road will be of little consequence when
I reach past the night and feel the light.

And the sun's warm glow wrapped around me.

Daylight

Sleepless, I don't have to be afraid. Stealing light from the stars. In the silence, still.

Waiting for a better day to come my way. With no beginning. Nothing left to fear.

Thinking back to that day. Watching time pass away. Feeling it tumble over me.

Listening to the sound of the voices inside of my head. Flowers still grow in the shade.

The vision of the face you once lived. It all seemed to disappear like it was never really there.

Watching daylight and the night skies. I don't want to let go. Tear drops, I'm drowning.

Hoping that I wake up. Beyond more. Shining a light.

Something even more beautiful

I let myself in. I left the keys inside the door.

I turned back the curtains and left the windows wide open.

Do you know I am here? In silence I wait.

I'm scared that my life got away. I am vaguely familiar.

In the darkness I am so afraid. My open wounds seem to never heal.

Instead of looking back, I have learned to trespass down the beaten path.

Sometimes the words get the best of me. I keep seeing someone else but it's not me.

There is no reason for you to cry. You are here. You give me hope.

You offer your hand, and we can start over again.

To become something even more beautiful.

November 2015

For my sons

Can I tell you something?

For all the times we looked to. For all the times we had.

When you have touched my heart and soul.

I will find myself in time for you. You are my whole world.

The time we share is eternal like the river that calls to the waterfalls — swirling around you, your tranquil aura shows.

Tonight under the starlight and for all the life we have given to each other, I will never find a moment like this time.

To have more time with you, my precious sons.

Chasing my tail

Trying to attach meaning to the crash is like trying to attach a tail to an invisible donkey.

It's frustrating to articulate to people — and that includes intelligent, sensible, educated and sympathetic friends and family — about what I'm going through, and why I can't just cheer up and snap out of it, that it's all in my head.

This entire accident experience just hurts. It's the precise inverse of joy and blots out pleasure at its whim, leaving a dull, faded outline of the happiness that was supposed to happen. It's also sneaky as hell.

So what am I afraid will happen? Presumably this is at the core of my recovery. There's no easy answer to that. My life is not easily explicable or rational. Since the accident I would describe my life as a free-floating, transformative fear that becomes all-consuming and often debilitating. For me, it's physically painful, from stomach, head and muscle aches to exhaustion from anxiety to raw and scabbed scalp spots that I've picked at until they bled — and kept picking some more.

I've been told it is time to 'feel' my pain rather than fight it or escape from it.

Gibson

Chapter 9

"It was a Catch-22: If you didn't put the trauma behind you, you couldn't move on. But if you did put the trauma behind you, you willingly gave up your claim to the person you were before it happened."

— Jodi Picoult

Life as we know it

Elie Wiesel, in his Nobel Peace Prize acceptance speech stated, "I remember: it happened yesterday, or eternities ago."

Life, as we know it, can change in a minute. Someone is born, someone passes on. Your home is full of young children. Before you know it they have all grown up. And these events change you.

The accident on September 18, 2013, has shifted me to a place I don't even know how to live in yet.

Time has taken its toll, and the aftermath of the accident has etched its mark on my mind, and with it has come an indelible mark on my life. Bits and pieces of the beautiful stained-glass work of art that had once been me has fallen away a bit at a time, leaving shards of metal and glass scattered all over me and my family.

I used to recognize myself. Perhaps it is time to finally walk away.

Time and life may take away what I may have known, that which I can see and touch, but it cannot touch the happy, glowing memories of what my life was — the presence which is so deeply implanted in the very core of my soul.

And this is what I hold near to my heart these days.

The dilemma

I woke up this morning with the conscious or unconscious desire for safety and control.

It's been easy to see that my own mind can feel like a minefield and staying safe sometimes requires escaping my memories and my life by suppressing them at any cost.

The use of medications and alcohol have in part made my life tolerable and have given me some semblance of control and the ability to soothe the fear, pain, shame and anxiety I feel.

But are they not just stopping me from feeling what I should be experiencing?

Therein lies my dilemma. To feel `my pain, fear, depression, anxiety, shame and guilt or, to manage these feelings and responses so I can tolerate them and process what happened so that I can move forward.

December 2015

The art of healing

Do you remember me? I'm just a shadow now.

I have fallen from a distant star, destined to come back because of our love.

I am caught between two different worlds. Lost within my own fading light.

You remain within my dreams? That's how I found you.

Sometimes I call out your name. Will you take a leap of faith with me?

What I would give to be lost in your eternal embrace.

If for every step I take toward the light on the path of this life, then surely I must leave a footprint for you to follow.

For I must at least try, as a keeper of stories, to find it deep within myself to take as many steps as possible.

The threshold

I was sleeping on the edge, a world somewhere, painted in the sky.

Within a meadow calm and serene.

A moment simply flutters at the edge of a dream.

I was shaken by a whisper. It only took a moment.

Somebody's out there. Your presence holds me back. It gives your name away.

I always remember. The point of no return. If I could just be set free.

In truth, I'm still feeling like I'm hanging in the air. Like a whisper.

I know you, I'm with you. The tears flowing down your beautiful face.

Time goes by. There are times I don't try.

Am I strong enough to learn?

Reach for me. We'll be safe and sound.

These are our reasons to believe.

Elusive

All I am. All I know.

I know not why, I know not how.

How it is, yet it is. No mystery solved. To explain these feelings inside.

I tell myself we can live a better life. Remembering when life felt whole.

Skies were always clear, and bright.

As you and I walked along the horizon and watched the sky fade away into the night.

We were swept away.

It was etched in the sand.

Why then is the tide closing in?

The fear of washing away.

I feel icy thoughts run through me — cold.

I keep the pain of a broken mind with wounds that just won't heal.

The Other Side of Reason

I'm falling deeper.

And I can't seem to find my way.

I have been doing circles in the places I hide.

But I keep trying to tell you.

It's a testimony to you — I look into your eyes and I find the truth.

If you take my hand I will ask for your forgiveness.
　　One more time.

Until the sunrise,

I will always come back to you.

January 2016

The incomprehensible haunting

Words on paper, I find, can't fully describe the experience of the accident. Yet somehow I am able to articulate how I feel infinitely better than through the spoken word. It is a paradox not lost on me.

I think there are few links between describing trauma in words and paving out an idea of meaning to cope with traumatic experiences. Too often, it seems there is silence around the trauma suffered by countless individuals who are living with the aftermath. I believe that the lived experience of trauma demands to be heard. It can have so many manifestations like nightmares, flashbacks, sexual and social dysfunction, and self-destructive behaviours like substance misuse or loss of impulse control.

What's different about writing or talking about trauma with these other harmful expressions? I believe that there's slightly more consent in the voicing of trauma. It is more palatable and seemingly less in your face. I believe it guarantees that as a survivor, I have a stake in my identity and self, in relation to what others may have also experienced.

By articulating my lived experience of trauma within my journal writings, I believe it also provides me a safe space to demand acknowledgement that there are reasons why my and family's life has been altered.

I realize that in trying to find meaning or even justice, it does not necessarily translate to being cured of the trauma nor of the anguish I live with today.

There's a line of poetry by Alexander Kimel, 'I Have to Remember and Never Let You Forget'. He's a survivor of the Holocaust, and I suppose for him, preserving the memorial in one's memory is a legitimate means of forging a kind of meaning in an altered existence.

Translating trauma into common language is similar to translating meaning into hope; it doesn't widely address everything going on, but it points to a way of connecting lived experience to the collective experience of others who have also survived.

I think this link between the individual and the 'collective' is essential to describing and finding meaning for myself to really 'let go', to move on.

The face of change

Words aren't so easy to share.

The act of bearing witness to traumatic events not only transforms traumatic memories into narratives that can be integrated into one's sense of self and view of the world, but it also has the potential to reintegrate you into a community, re-establishing bonds of trust and faith in others.

That is of course, if you are able to find your voice and a community that will listen to you and accept you as a person that matters.

Time may be perceived as linear, but from my perspective, the aftermath of the crash was not. There have been many periods since the accident of progress and of decline, victories and setbacks, both major and minor. I have changed since September 18, 2013 and so have my views, but, rather than revise my earlier journal writings in light of my recovery journey, I have tried to convey the trajectory of my ideas and feelings of living with trauma. As Ursula LeGuin describes, "it doesn't seem right or wise to revise an old text severely, as if trying to obliterate it, hiding the evidence that one had to go from there to get here". For me it is rather to let those changes of mind, and the process of change, stand as evidence.

To a large extent, I believe we're the keepers of each other's stories about this tragedy, and the shape of these stories has unfolded in part from our own interwoven accounts. Eva Hoffman considers these interconnections as a "process of where we don't only search for meanings, we are ourselves units of meaning; but we can mean something only within in the fabric of later significances".

Trauma, however, unravels whatever meaning we've found and wove ourselves into, and so listening to stories like mine is an experience in unlearning.

Trauma I believe severely impairs your ability to be connected to humanity in ways that you value.

So what is the goal of being a survivor? Ultimately I believe, it is not to transcend the trauma, not to solve the dilemmas of everyday living, but simply to endure.

February 2016

The things I am learning

Time after time the human spirit has had many attempts to test its strength and I've seen where it has not been broken. That's me in the mirror. I am not broken, but I am, piecing my life back together.

Things that happen to us hurt, I know. I would not be pretentious enough to sit here and write about rainbows and flowers when life can be so ugly and mean. I've been there. I am still here.

I intellectually get it — allowing your emotions will not hurt you. It heals you. The battles I am experiencing in dealing with the after effects of the accident are in direct conflict with what I am experiencing with flashbacks, intrusions, anxiety attacks, nightmares and the numbness I feel.

This conflicting dynamic has been highlighted in the philosophy of Eckhart Tolle. He basically says that it's not the things that happen to you from which your pain arises, but your reaction to it. From his perspective, I believe his message is that to feel, is to invite the pain, fear, shame and guilt into our lives and grow.

I am also trying to learn how to make my past part of my future. I know I can't change what happened over two years ago, but I am trying to decide how I can interpret and respond to the aftermath.

Living with trauma is essentially a challenge to who you are as a person and one that takes you and everyone you care for, on an emotional roller-coaster ride.

I am learning that sometimes there are no short cuts. The hardest thing to do is to forgive yourself and the past. If it is true, forgiveness won't only resolve my past, but it should alleviate any fear of my future. I think for now there is a gap for me between the place I am in now and the place I want to be.

The truth of forgiveness will be freestanding, not just dependent upon faith, but upon my belief in humanity. The 'real' truth is that I must forgive myself in order to be able to forgive why a preventable accident happened. This journey is a decision that I must make in order to forgive the unforgivable.

Until then I am also learning that its okay to forgive yourself for not being ready.

March 2016

Finding my way back

The power of trauma often lies in the shame and guilt it leaves with people. This shame or guilt lasts and lingers in the body, mind, in the silences that accompany them, and in the way we consequently view ourselves.

I often wonder if my journal is nothing more than an escape from wanting to change. What difference will writing make? Does it even really matter? And honestly, after reading what I have written, I often wondered, "What point am I making?"

Yet no matter how I feel, my journal entries always meet me where I am and have the power to help me transform from one point in time to the next.

I have found that writing can also offer healing, reassurances, hopefulness, insight, and like songs, are a powerful container for strong emotions which can help bring new perspectives and clarity into my life. I have also experienced the connections with others who have experienced trauma when I see and hear words composed by another. There's an important shared connection: someone else has been there and come through the other side.

I believe the difference between where I am now and where I can be, is hope. Sometimes hope is all I have. Perhaps it is through these connections with others that I can overcome where I am now — feeling unsure of what is going to happen after the accident or how I am ever going to climb out of the darkness and regain my life.

Lived experiences, human connections

When we wake up from our night-time dreams, do we wake up into 'reality' or do we go to sleep into a dream, which we all call reality?

An existential conundrum I am living with.

If the definition of poetry stops at 'writing that expresses emotion', then poetry can be therapeutic. I am not trying to write myself into some form of curative stability. At best, my journal may confront the void, articulate fears, challenge the notion of justice, channel grief, and tell stories; but I began writing for reasons beyond just therapeutic expression. I began to write my own story, but also found that my story was one within many others' fears, loss, and pain.

What takes my journal beyond the "merely" therapeutic is my determination to make the journal communicate as a collection of poems rather than as an expression of just my individual traumatic experience. Therapy I have found can release, relieve, or comfort, but poetry expands my relationship to the broad continuum of human lives over countless lived experiences.

Therapy isn't meant to do that, and should not. It is a different kind of endeavor.

My promise through my writing is to transcend whatever it is that makes that connection to another human being possible.

My hope is I have done this both for myself and for you.

Inspiration

My journal is an attempt I believe, at finding hope because I know the threat of being consumed by fear, anger and pain. I have shared real struggles with ambiguity and damaged words, because I have been bruised and battered internally. And truthfully, living with trauma takes its toll on the mind as well.

Somewhere along the way I have realized I will need to find some space to pursue hope and inspire some measure of meaning out of this tragic experience.

Certainly my writing has evolved and I suspect it will continue to do so because the healing journey I am on is not over. Much of my healing to come will be about the pursuit of hope and meaning, and continuing to write with this focus, may in fact, answer the significant 'so what' question.

I remember being asked once if I was a pessimist or an optimist. I replied, "That depends". The reality is that there are times when I really struggle to see the good in things, and there are times when I'm not only seeing them, but optimistic to share that good with others.

Only by living with trauma, experiencing and understanding, accepting and seeing — really seeing, what I have lived, what I know, what I feel, can I be free of the demons. It is in my pain that I believe humanity lies, not in the laughter and joy of success, but in the pain of sadness and loss.

Is this my truth?

I am more than what I think I am and this truth is part of my recovery journey.

April 2016

Winter's escape

From the top of the hill for as far as our eyes can see, palm trees, white-washed sand and rolling surf.

My heart races as I watch your smiling face take in our new piece of Caribbean heaven.

The blue and green hues of the ocean sparkles in the sun's warm rays.

Overhead pelicans and terns greet us with their welcome calls.

Hand in hand we follow the shoreline path of the sandpipers, running in and out of the surf.

Eternal, our hearts capture the moment we have become one.

Tidal pool

I am in a tidal pool, watching everybody else around me effortlessly swimming toward the shallow end while I'm desperately trying to swim my way out of the deep end.

No matter how hard I try, I never seem to get further than from where I started.

Why is it that nobody seems to see me trying?

May 2016

Memories in the closet

On a hanger, a reminder of dark memories from another time and place.

Hanging in the closet, perfectly preserved, is a blue jacket.

Not just any jacket though. This jacket fits perfectly on the ghost of my mind.

A time that is frozen with my body standing still and trapped.

Shivering from the cold autumn air the blue jacket screams out the pain, fear and anger I feel.

My hands shake as I reach for the blue jacket.

The blue jacket is preserved just like the nightmares that haunt me.

Slipping the blue jacket off the hanger, a stark realization makes me feel sick.

I have so much hatred toward this blue jacket, or perhaps it is towards myself.

Once I am united with this blue jacket, what then?

After all, it's just — a blue jacket.

When I open my eyes

The disconnect lies in the mirror.

All I have is this feeling inside of me.

Maybe right now and right here I am as close to life as one can possibly be.

To allow myself to feel it all. To allow myself to be finally free.

To gently let myself go.

This moment no longer belongs to me.

Time to slow it down.

A few minutes more and I will see.

What freedom brings when I open my eyes.

Paddling away from the edge

Dawn on the lake. Another season begins. The world is still. The water is like a mirror. Land and water blur. Bold bright colors shine in the morning light.

Steam rises from the still surface in wisps and swirls, soon to evaporate in the warming air. The paddle bites into the tawny depths. Shafts of light illuminate the newborn waves.

A ribbon of water streams off the blade. I am paddling silently to hold onto the stillness.

The call of the morning loon brings forth my return to this lake.

Another day, I am here.

Homeward embrace

When the night disappears you are always there.

You pull me from the darkness.

Come fill up my senses with you.

I wish I was back where I belong.

In dawn's time of different coloured lights.

Worlds away I am spinning.

I'd risk my life just to feel anything but nothing.

The way that I am carrying this around,
   it's heavy on my shoulders.

Searching for a better way to find my way home
   to your smile.

I wonder when I will have arrived.

Is there any way that I can stay?

Where time is frozen still.

Where spring's blossoms make me feel brand new.

Reflections from afar

I am the one who has inherited your eyes.

I have heard what you have seen.

I am the witness to your experience.

You are no longer alone.

I know you're scared. Don't be.

Because the world really is beautiful.

Turn the hourglass upside down

There is a call to the present.

The here and now.

The limitlessness in being someone and something.

Like an unceasing, surging heart preserving life.

I hold still to find the space inside.

I must have been in this place before, yet I look so brand-new.

I am coming to terms with the fright of my mind.

I finally realize I always had that palace of peace and love within myself.

Inside the bottle

Suddenly darkness overflows.

Fear rushes through my veins.

Images still echoing through my mind.

I stumble and fall. Everything swirling around me. My god, I am on the bathroom floor.

If I could just get back up — I can't feel myself.

No escaping this ignited pain and fear. I have locked myself in.

But I can't seem to break free. I need someone. Why is this hole so deep and cold?

I'm getting hit by the crash so hard.

Right now, I am slowly falling apart. Tearing out your heart. I know you are scared.

Fighting fiercely, desperately with the demons inside my head.

Inside I am screaming. But wait, my anguished cries have already left my head.

The Other Side of Reason

Am I nothing more than a memory?

Just a person who you used to know?

Someone who depended on the strength that lies within.

I am a wounded warrior trying to grasp at that last ounce of strength to not give in — you must never give in.

Hiding my thoughts secretly. It's just a memory that's all.

I am fading, slipping away.

But still, I am whispering — maybe I am mumbling, I can't be sure.

It is just a memory…

June 2016

The art of becoming

The sun is rising and there is no more compromising.

Passing from illusion to illusion. The fracture is in time.

So many tiny echoes remain.

Those gone-forever eyes. They have taken the stars
   from me.

Your presence is swift though, coming and going as quickly
   as the thoughts that enter my mind in those quiet
   moments before falling asleep.

When I am jolted back into reality, I wonder what that
   moment was, that foreboding sense of being neither
   here nor there.

Just somewhere, not in a daydream or a nightmare,
   not in the awakened state nor in the sleep state.
   I am here.

The clearest reflection mirrors my new horizon.
   I'm looking straight ahead.

I am becoming someone different.

And releasing you to the summer's warm breeze.

Awakening from a dream of sunrise

As I journey toward the dawn always moving,
    always still.

Slivers of light break through blankets of clouds.

I am at a threshold, between wakefulness and sleep,
    darkness and the dawn, the stillness and the song.

The waters of the lake are still, its luminescence hidden
    in fog that hugs the waterline and shrouds the world
    in silence.

There is no road to walk across the lake...

No easy trail on which to stand.

Yet even here, especially here, love is present in the
    surrounding silent beauty.

I've entered a land of newborn possibility.

No fences, no boundaries hem me in.

Clarity is now mine...intense blue sky.

Warm sun against distant shores.

Only surreal stillness marks this place.

Where I am awakening from a dream of sunrise.

The legacy proposition

In the distance, I hear a train rolling away.

There's sorrow in my soul that will only cease with
  breath itself.

I know it's there... motionless as death.

It seeks no healing, asks for no aid.

Vainly would I strive to vanquish, attempt to cleanse
  or drive it away.

Every day is still a winding and irregular stone path,
  walking down the labyrinth of my past.

It's heavier, deeper, longer than I expected,
  where countless shadows still lurk.

I can see a refreshed vision unfolding, burning the long,
  dark night away.

A breeze blows from nearby lake shores, unseen,
  busy swallowing all that the river brings.

In the pale morning light of summer.

July 2016

Illumination

Shooting stars cross the canopy of the night.

Following the Milky Way there seems to be no beginning nor end to the path in the midnight sky.

I walk through the illumination of my life and count my strides.

I let my feet receive the scars that only a long journey can promise. But I can never let the scars stop me from taking one step, and then another.

Until I find myself nestled by the curve of the moon.

I am the breeze

The first shafts of sunlight pierce the darkness.

From the rose bushes a sparrow's song echoes among the rippled shadows.

I am the breeze.

Passing through the willow leaves with a single gesture of goodbye.

Memories come flooding back.

Buried in the depths. A fragment here. A shard there.

It's not the end, it's a new beginning.

Just as the seasons pass by.

I am the breeze that continues on.

To weather emotions through time

In summer I unravel the machinations of time.

I walk to where the river runs fast and breathless over solemn stones.

Can anybody hear, like I, the ceaseless song of the water.

Light dances mischievously on the surface as the sun does not set, but slips willingly behind the shadow of dusk.

The trees are calmed, and I unfold myself from the silky earth.

As the river continues its melody, I listen to the exquisite music of nature's nightly procession.

The moon bears silent witness

As twilight enters my somber room, I brush away the dreams.

Memories rush into my mind, and I reach out to find empty space.

These recollections I can no longer face.

The stress on my world crushes my soul.

I don't want to lose myself again.

Let there be peace.

Let the darkness come.

I call upon your requiem.

With half shut eyes I stare into the silent shining moon.

And a myriad of stars sparkle bright chasing away my midnight gloom.

August 2016

Skimming along the surface

The sun struck the water surface like a metallic sheen.

Speeding by like a bird in a boundless sky.

Skimming along the surface I tread lightly.

Avoiding my confronting deeper fears.

It's hard to live while stuck on the water's edge.

And living on life's outer edge.

Each step is another at the end of all others,

Never far from the currents of tomorrow.

Bridge of life

Some days I worry I'm growing hollow.

I'm filled with the things I've seen and what I know.

I don't want to get to the end of anything anymore. I only want beginnings.

The crazy fool that dances in the rain.

This hot summer evening I escape to be in a different place.

The entire lake before me is mirrored.

Offering me space to hope that by some crazy miracle, you will hold my hand and listen to the beauty of my heart and soul.

Reminiscence

Wheat fields ripple, bounce back and forth, anticipating.

I move unhampered by the flirting breeze.

My past recedes; my future quietly rests.

If darkness should ever overwhelm me.

All you have to do is listen clearly.

Remember me as one who sought solace in the rainbow of memories.

And did not bow to the panoramic temptation of the evening skies.

Dew drops and sunshine

It is a sight, a feeling and place I shall never,
   not in my life, or any other, want to know.

Each day is the only day.

Like daffodils in daylight, to bloom.

The glistening dew drops, a spectrum of morning's dawn.

A chance to see. A chance to shine.

And a chance to be free.

September 2016

Where the past meets the present

Looking down at the ground, my eyes trace the pattern of the fallen leaves that blanket the ground.

The dark earth contrasts their fading fall colours.

Among the leaves rests a single yellow rose. Where it came from, I do not know.

Water droplets caress the rose from the morning's dew and offer a radiance to the new day's early light.

Was it put there as a memory to the past, or to a start of a new day?

Can the yellow rose embody a new meaning and beginning?

I touch the delicate petals understanding the intricate balance of its beauty and meaning.

A wish for our wellbeing today, and for all of our tomorrows, and bidding adieu to the fallen leaves of September.

Gibson

Epilogue

I always have this reflection about how we are living our lives, and then something happens in an instant that has consequences we live with for the rest of our lives.

Because of the writing I have done over the past three years, I am acutely aware that the journey of healing will be very different for anyone who has experienced trauma. And some, a very small percentage, will need long-term intervention to travel this journey. There is never a "correct" way that we should feel trauma; rather, there is the way that we experience trauma.

I would say that anything that is life threatening can be life changing. There are different ways in which we can change or grow, but the likelihood of growth is tremendous if we have people who support us, encourage us and walk beside us. It is also critical that the people who are beside us give us the permission to feel the way we feel. And even if those feelings are quite negative or hurtful to ourselves, or to others, that we still provide a safe place for people to work through those feelings.

We need allies, rather than having people telling us what we must do — that we should feel this way or that way or even to just move on.

I think trauma raises questions about our fragility as human beings — our vulnerability, but also our mortality, and this can be quite distressing for some people. And for me, it still is central to my recovery.

Another key element to my journey, is the understanding that relinquishing control, or letting go, can be a form of regaining control. This book publicly acknowledges this.

Together our stories matter. Together our voices matter. Mine is not an exception, rather it is just another voice that binds us all together. Our voices are the expressions of our humanity and our journey of living within this life.

It has not been easy to share my feelings, but, for me, this book follows one of the many pathways to recovery and presents a vehicle to help spread the important messages about sharing and managing our mental wellbeing.

This book is about being honest with how I feel, and, in many ways, the writing process has helped in reducing my isolation and even diminished some of the emotional impact of the accident. I never thought I would end up like this in my life time. My hope is that my writing will help others express how they feel.

The chances are good that many people who read these journal entries will relate to them immediately. Although their experiences will no doubt be different, I am finding a universality of experience among the people I have spoken to and the cases of which I have read.

In silence we will not heal.

Courage is our ability to bring that lived experience of trauma out of the shadows and into the public discourse on mental health issues. Because our stories do matter, and will always matter. Courage will be an important asset in taking those first steps.

So what happens beyond story telling? What does healing look like, or even feel like?

The Other Side of Reason

This is the part in the book where I am to shine my great insights, wisdom and tie everything into a pretty bow. I wish I could, I really do. But it doesn't always work that way in life. Not entirely anyway. It is not to say that I am not learning or even trying to imagine or build an ambitious existential purpose for my place in the world. It's just that healing takes time and my expectations have become much more modest and incremental rather than grandiose.

Someone once asked me after previewing this book: is your life really like this? Retrospection it seems can also illuminate little nuggets of lived experience to answer questions like these.

I learned about the depths of despair and the cruelty of sudden loss. But I also learned that when life pulls me under, I can kick and scream against the bottom, break the surface, and take a breath again. I learned that in the face of the dark chasm I can still choose to learn and re-build a life bridge that reinforces purpose and resilience once more.

I have learned to believe that my ability to recover comes from hoping I will recover in some way, if not entirely. Knowing that my emotional distress will always coexist with my capacity to grow and learn, also helps to alleviate frustration and anger.

The ability to keep trying even when times are difficult, helps me reach beyond myself and discover new possibilities and meaning within my life. This in turn allows for new perspectives and behaviours to help with regulating my emotional responses, tolerate anxiety, manage stress and develop coping skills or mindfulness techniques.

I have learned to remember who I still am as a person. Memories, I have found, can only tell me who I once was.

Beyond these little nuggets of lived experience, I am still in the process of trying to re-anchor who I am.

I'm sharing this with you in the hopes that as you take the next courageous steps in your life, you can learn the lessons that I only learned through surviving a horrible bus crash. Lessons about hope, strength, and the light within us that will never be extinguished.

Am I able to re-imagine my life in a positive way? The key I believe is to find meaning in life, rather than the meaning of life. With PTSD you tend to be incoherent, fragmented and stuck on negative memories. I have tended to describe myself as "a hostage of the past", "empty inside", "a shell", "not worthy", or "sleepwalking through my life".

But what if I were to spin another version of my story, one that includes an account of how I survived, how I managed to get the mental health support I needed, and the path I have been able to follow since that horrible accident. This story would be coherent, forward-looking and one that joins my past to my future.

It would be story which says that surviving trauma is not only about recovery but also about growth. Sometimes great suffering can lead to a transformation of self—a transformation that has the potential to wake me to the deep questions of life.

And once aware of those questions, I would finally believe anything is possible.

The Other Side of Reason

Here's what readers are saying (continued)

"September 18, 2013, what started as a normal fall day changed lives of many in matter of few seconds due to a 'preventable accident' that claimed six lives and left many invisibly injured for life. David Gibson, a regular passenger on that bus route, experiences the trauma and searches his way out of the deep anguish, trying to reclaim his life and become himself again. Through this reflective journal, he takes us on this journey along with him. We feel his pain, his hurt and then his search for some meaning and hope that he will be whole again. This process makes us, the readers, more understanding of people who have been through trauma."

— Hersh Sehdev

"In this compelling and easy-to-read book, David Gibson shares in an honest and courageous manner how he has coped with the aftermath of being a passenger on a commuter bus involved in a tragic accident. The book is a must-read for trauma survivors and those close to them, mental health professionals, and anyone else interested in understanding the powerful impact of trauma in a person's life. It brings to light in a personal and in-depth manner the daily challenges associated with surviving and making sense of a traumatic event, something many of us will encounter during our lifetime".

— Tim Aubry

"David has written a powerful description of the journey through trauma from an intensely personal perspective. It opened my eyes to the pain and uncertainty that was hidden below the surface that was visible to me. I wished my friend could have talked to me about what he was going through. I wished that I could have found a way to reach out to him. His writing has opened my eyes and I hope it will help others to understand the impact of tragic accidents on the survivors."

"When a good man is hurt, all who would be called good must suffer with him." (Euripides)

— George Acton

"A tragic bus accident ended the lives of six and changed the lives of eighty-six survivors forever. David Gibson takes us on an intimate and difficult journey of personal healing, sharing with us his struggles to come to terms with this horrific event and what it has meant for him to be one of those survivors. David's narrative opens wide a window into his changed world and new reality, sharing his pain, anger, uncertainty and emptiness, as well as his incredible courage, love and hope. I am profoundly grateful to David for giving me the opportunity to glance through this window."

— Eric Crighton

Gibson

Illustrations

Cover	Orange leaves. dreamstime.com © Barbara Helgason
Frontispiece	Train tracks. istock gettyimages © tomasworks
Contents	Trees above. dreamstime.com © Szefei
Chapter 1	Hands on glass. dreamstime.com © Lasse Behnke
Chapter 2	Walking in fog. dreamstime.com © Melinda Nagy
Chapter 3	Holding knees. dreamstime.com © Gloria-leigh
Chapter 4	Driving. dreamstime.com © Alex Grichenko
Chapter 5	Couple on beach. dreamstime.com © Anyaberkut
Chapter 6	Walking on beach. dreamstime.com © Ileanaolaru
Chapter 7	Clock. dreamstime.com © Chikapylka
Chapter 8	Open book dreamstime.com © Carmen Steiner
Chapter 9	Avenue of trees. dreamstime.com © Aleksey Locshilov
Epilogue	Walking. dreamstime.com © Gajus
Endpiece	Rose on leaves. gettyimages, credit Orlin Bertsch
Facing page	Leaves in wind. dreamstime.com © Marsia16

Passages

		page
Addair, George	businessman	92
Anon	first responder	iii
Becker, Ernest	psychologist	5
Euripides	playwright	207
Gibson, Andrea	poet	21
Hamilton, Laurell K.	writer	77
Hoffman, Eva	academic	169
Kimel, Alexander	poet	167
LeGuin, Ursula	writer	168
Morris, David J.	writer	109
Ostriker, Alicia	poet	136
Palahniuk, Chuck	writer	127
Pease Banitt, Susan	therapist	37
Picoult, Jodi	writer	159
Stern, Jessica	academic	49
Tolle, Eckhart	writer	170
Wiesel, Elie	writer	160
Winfrey, Oprah	media	61

www.ingramcontent.com/pod-product-compliance
Lightning Source LLC
Chambersburg PA
CBHW031148020426
42333CB00013B/559